Hebrew Bible or Old Testament?

Christianity and Judaism in Antiquity
Charles Kannengiesser, S. J., Series Editor

Volume 5

Hebrew Bible

or

Old Testament?

Studying the Bible
in
Judaism and Christianity

Edited by

ROGER BROOKS
and
JOHN J. COLLINS

University of Notre Dame Press
Notre Dame, Indiana

Cover: אחת דבר אלהים שתים־זו שמעתי כי עז לאלהים
One thing God has spoken, two things have I heard;
that might belongs to God (Ps. 62:12)

Library of Congress Cataloging-in-Publication Data

Hebrew Bible or Old Testament? : Studying the Bible in Judaism and
Christianity / edited by Roger Brooks and John J. Collins.
    p.   cm. — (Christianity and Judaism in antiquity ; v. 5)
Includes bibliographical references.
ISBN 0-268-01090-0
    1. Bible. O.T.—Criticism, interpretation, etc.—History—20th century. 2.
Bible. O.T.—Criticism, interpretation, etc., Jewish—History—20th century.
3. Bible O.T.—Terminology. I. Brooks, Roger. II. Collins, John Joseph,
1946-   . III. Series.
221.6'07—dc20   89-40749

In Remembrance of
Etta and Bert Liss
whose dedication to the University of Notre Dame
supported education and excellence in Jewish-Christian
relations.

זכרון צדקים לברכה

Contents

Part One: What's in a Name? The Problem of What We Study

Part Two: The Theological Costs of Historical-Critical Study

Acknowledgments

The papers contained here were first presented at the 1989 University of Notre Dame Conference, *Hebrew Bible or Old Testament? Studying the Bible in Judaism and Christianity.* The conference was made possible by generous support from the Department of Theology, its Crown-Minow Fund for Programs in Jewish-Christian Relations, and the College of Arts and Letters.

The editors extend special thanks to Richard P. McBrien, Chairman of the Department of Theology, and to F. Ellen Weaver, Asistant Chairwoman of the Department of Theology, for their guidance and aid.

This volume is dedicated to Etta and Bert Liss, devoted patrons of the Department of Theology at the University of Notre Dame. The volumes inspired by their thoughtful support would fill a library.

Contributors

JOSEPH BLENKINSOPP, John A. O'Brien Professor of Biblical Studies at the University of Notre Dame, was born in England and has taught at institutions on both sides of the Atlantic. He served as rector of the Ecumenical Institute near Jerusalem and as codirector of the excavation on the Greek Orthodox site at Capernaum, Israel (1980-1987). His most recent publications are commentaries on Ezra-Nehemiah (Old Testament Library series) and on Ezekiel (forthcoming Spring 1990 with Westminster/John Knox Press).

ROGER BROOKS is Assistant Professor of Judaic Studies in the Department of Theology at the University of Notre Dame. In addition to interests in Jewish-Christian relations, his research focuses on the theology of early rabbinic Judaism. He is author of *The Spirit of the Ten Commandments: Shattering the Myth of Rabbinic Legalism* (Harper and Row, 1990) and *The Talmud of the Land of Israel, Tractate Peah* (University of Chicago Press, 1990).

ADELA YARBRO COLLINS is Professor of New Testament in the Department of Theology at the University of Notre Dame. She is currently at work on a commentary on the Gospel of Mark for the Hermeneia series. She is author of *Crisis and Catharsis: The Power of the Apocalypse* (Westminster Press), *The Apocalypse* (Michael Glazier, Inc.), and editor of *Feminist Perspectives on Biblical Scholarship* (Scholars Press). Professor Collins has been the editor of the Society of Biblical Literature Monograph Series since 1985.

JOHN J. COLLINS teaches in the Department of Theology at the University of Notre Dame and is editor of the *Journal of Biblical Literature*. His books include *Between Athens and Jerusalem: Jewish Identity in the Hellenistic Diaspora* (Crossroad, 1983); *The Apocalyptic Imagination* (Crossroad,

1984); and *Daniel, With an Introduction to Apocalyptic Literature* (Eerdmans, 1984). He is coeditor of the *Oxford Catholic Study Bible* (Oxford University Press, 1990).

JOSEPHINE MASSYNGBAERDE FORD is Professor of New Testament at the University of Notre Dame. Her interest in Judaism and the New Testament has been longstanding and was kindled by David Daube, Professor of Law at the University of California, Berkeley. Her recent books include *My Enemy is My Guest* (Orbis Press, 1984) and *Bonded with the Immortal: A Pastoral Introduction to the New Testament* (Michael Glazier, 1987).

CHARLES E. KANNENGIESSER, S.J., Catherine F. Huisking Professor of Theology at the University of Notre Dame, lectures on early Christian Literature and Christology. A member of the Institute for Advanced Study, Princeton, New Jersey, he focuses his research on the biography of Athanasius of Alexandria. He serves currently as president of the North American Patristics Society.

JAMES L. KUGEL is the Starr Professor of Hebrew Literature, Harvard University. He is author of *The Idea of Biblical Poetry* (Yale University Press, 1981), *Early Biblical Interpretation* (Westminster, 1986), and of the forthcoming *In Potiphar's House* (Harper and Row, 1990) and *Poetry and Prophecy* (Cornell University Press, 1990). He currently is preparing a collection of texts illustrating how various passages in the Hebrew Bible were interpretaed in early Judaism and Christianity.

DAVID LEVENSON is Associate Professor of Religion at Florida State University. He received his Ph. D. from Harvard University in New Testament and Christian Origins. His present area of research is in Jewish, Christian, and Pagan relations in late antiquity. His book, *Julian and Jerusalem: The Sources and the Tradition*, is to be published by E. J. Brill. He has been active in Jewish-Christian dialogue for the past twenty-five years and with his colleague John Kelsay has recently published "Double Talk or Dialogue? Presbyterians Encounter Judaism" in *The Christian Century*.

JON D. LEVENSON is the Albert A. List Professor of Jewish Studies in the Divinity School and the Department of Near Eastern Languages and Civilizations at Harvard University. His most recent books are *Sinai and Zion: An Entry into the Jewish Bible* and *Creation and the Persistence of Evil: The Jewish Drama of Divine Omnipotence*, both published by Harper and Row. He has also served as associate editor of the new Harper's Bible Commentary.

ROLAND E. MURPHY, O. CARM., is the George Washington Ivey Emeritus Professor of Biblical Studies at Duke University and now teaches at the Washington Theological Union. His research has focused on biblical wisdom literature, and he is contributor and coeditor of *The New Jerome Biblical Commentary* (1990). In 1985 he was the John A. O'Brien Visiting Professor of Theology at the University of Notre Dame.

ROLF RENDTORFF is Professor for Old Testament Studies at the University of Heidelberg. Deeply influenced by his teacher, Gerhard von Rad, over several decades he has studied problems of Jewish-Christian relations, particularly their consequences for interpretation of the Hebrew Bible. He is author of *The Old Testament: An Introduction* (Fortress Press, 1985) and is now working on a commentary to the Book of Leviticus and on different preparatory studies toward a theology of the Old Testament.

JAMES A. SANDERS teaches at the Institute for Antiquity and Christianity at the Claremont School of Theology and is a former president of the Society for Biblical Literature. His publications include *The Psalms Scroll of Qumran Cave 11, Discoveries in the Judean Desert, 4* (Oxford Unviersity Press, 1965); *Torah and Canon* (Fortress Press, 1972); and *From Sacred Story to Sacred Text: Canon as Paradigm* (Fortress Press, 1987).

EUGENE ULRICH is Professor of Hebrew Scriptures at the University of Notre Dame and Fellow of the Institute for Advanced Studies at the Hebrew University of Jerusalem for 1989-1990. He is the chief editor of the biblical scrolls from Qumran Cave 4, author of *The Qumran Text of Samuel and Josephus* and of numerous editions of biblical manuscripts and articles on the text of the Scriptures and the history of the biblical text. He is president of the International Organization for Septuagint and Cognate Studies and was appointed to the Bible Revision Committee of the National Council of Churches for *The Holy Bible: New Revised Standard Version* and to the revision committee for the *New American Bible* Psalter.

Introduction

ROGER BROOKS AND JOHN J. COLLINS

The Christian appropriation of the Hebrew Scriptures has become a sensitive issue in recent years.[1] Jewish scholars have pointed out that supposedly objective treatments of the religion and history of Israel have often been profoundly biased by Christian theological presuppositions.[2] An increasing number of Christian scholars concede the justice of the complaint:[3] the traditional supersessionist claim that biblical religion finds its true fulfillment in Christianity has undeniably led to the denigration of Judaism, ancient, medieval, and modern, and cannot be held innocent of the outrage of anti-Semitism and Holocaust in our century. Concession of this point has considerable implications for Christian theology, for supersessionism is deeply rooted in that tradition. Nonetheless, it is a presupposition of the dialogue presented in this volume that a supersessionist view of the Old Testament is no longer tenable.

---

1. See the essays in Boadt, Croner, and Klenicki, *Biblical Studies*; see also Klopfenstein, Luz, Talmon, and Tov, *Mitte der Schrift*. Full references to works cited throughout this volume are found below, in the General Bibliography.
2. See especially Levenson, "Hebrew Bible, the Old Testament, and Historical Criticism," 19-59; and Levenson, "Why Jews Are Not Interested," 281-307.
3. Blenkinsopp, "Old Testament Theology," 3-15.

One manifestation of the nonsupersessionist reading of Scripture is found in the interfaith ecumenical movement, which has promoted better relations between Jews and Christians by making popular the claim that the Old Testament (also: Hebrew Bible, *Tanakh*, or simply Jewish Scripture, the Bible) is Scripture that we Jews and Christians share. So, it is alleged, in the first few centuries of our era, both fledgling religions interpreted and expounded the same books, from Genesis to Chonicles, from Amos to Zechariah. If each religious group had its preferences for certain books or passages as opposed to others, at least some agreement could be found in the larger construct, the Bible.[4]

The essays presented in this volume address three separate issues. First: What is the literature we study? How do we delimit its scope and meaning, and even its title? Second: How shall we combine religious attitudes toward the creation and interpretation of Scripture with historical-critical observations that challenge us not only because of their radically different assumptions about the Bible, but also because of their adherence to standards of historical method that most of us fully share? Third: What do some Jewish, Christian, and historical-critical readings of particular texts look like when juxtaposed to each other?

WHAT'S IN A NAME? THE PROBLEM OF WHAT WE STUDY

Many questions lurk behind the simple fact that we read the same books. What characterizes Jewish readings and interpretations of the *Tanakh*? Given the manner in which Judaic interpretations of the Bible are rooted in Jewish Law and theology, do those readings really share anything at all with

4. For examples of this resort to common Scripture, see Neusner, *Aphrahat and Judaism*, 4-7; and Wilken, *John Chrysostom and the Jews*, 124.

their Christian counterparts? The same questions, of course, apply on the Christian side: What defines Christian exegesis, and does it have a common element with Jewish interpretation? The meanings we assign to individual words, whole sentences, chapters, and even books, are largely a matter of communal agreement. That agreement, in turn, often emerges from the very heart of our most basic religious conceptions.

Christians, for instance, read what many of them call the Old Testament. According to recent Vatican pronouncements, that means the chronologically older Testament;[5] but sometimes Old Testament is meant to imply an out-of-date vision of God's relationship with humanity. In any case, this Testament is only part of the Christian Bible, and the New Testament impinges on the way the Old Testament is read. Jews, on the other hand, read the *Tanakh*, an acronym refering to the one and only Torah bearing God's Law (תורה), the exclusive and validated books of the Prophets (נביאים), and the other holy Writings (כתובים). They also have other authoritative books—the Mishnah, Talmuds, and Midrash-compilations—that shape their perception of the *Tanakh*.[6] Each religion has traditionally incorporated the biblical material into a theological system, and the two systems are incompatible at some fundamental points.

Various scholars have grappled with this problem of the identity and appropriate name for the Scriptures under discussion here. Roland E. Murphy, O. Carm., for example, would allow the two terms—Hebrew Bible, Old Testament—to stand, as long as the differences these names imply are clearly held in mind. So it is that divergent literary structures and contexts are conjured up—rightly—by the Judaic and Christian

5. See "Notes on the Correct Way to Present Jews and Judaism," 102-7.
6. See, e.g., Neusner and Green, *Authority and Uses of the Hebrew Bible.*

idioms. James A. Sanders, by contrast, would prefer to rename Scripture: Jews would read the First Testament; Christians both the First and Second Testaments. This terminology avoids the possible derogatory implications of *old*, but is still a distinctly Christian formulation: *first*, after all, implies that *second* is to follow. Rolf Rendtorff, for his part, embraces the Hebrew Bible as a fundamental basis for Christianity as for Judaism, and he defends the possibility of a common reading.

THE THEOLOGICAL COSTS OF HISTORICAL-CRITICAL STUDY

The abandonment of Christian supersessionist assumptions is a straightforward product of the Jewish-Christian dialogue; yet it is important to insist that this concession is not made only to facilitate such dialogue. The traditional Christian view of the Old Testament, typified by the attempt to find prophecies of Christ in the older Scriptures, has lost credibility for most Christians, and has been thoroughly undermined by historical criticism. Any Christian theology informed by modern biblical study must come to terms with the fact that the Hebrew Bible has its own integrity and is not in itself a Christian document. This realization may open up the possibility of finding common ground with Judaism, but it is unavoidable in any case.

Against this background, Rolf Rendtorff makes his proposal that the theology of the Hebrew Bible should be studied from within, on its own terms, free from the presuppositions of either rabbinic or Christian theology, a proposal he hopes is not utopian. The discussions in this volume, however, indicate considerable misgivings on this point. In this post-Gadamerian age we can no longer believe in the possibility of exegesis without presuppositions. In fact, Rendtorff's proposal has strong overtones of Reformation theology—the ideals of unmediated access to Scripture, on the one hand, and the self-sufficiency of Scripture (*sola scriptura*), on the other. Both ideals ask more of Scripture than it can yield. We inevitably bring to the text a specific communal setting for our biblical interpretation.[7] Rendtorff, like most scholars, operates with some form of historical criticism. It is important to realize and admit that what modern critical study yields is not simply "what the Bible says." It is "what the Bible says" from a particular perspective. Historical criticism cannot claim the unqualified authority of biblical revelation any more than traditional Jewish or Christian theology.[8]

Even so, there is much to be said for historical criticism as the best starting point for contemporary biblical theology.[9] It is of the essence of historical criticism that it rules out appeals to faith and demands evidence for the positions we take.[10] Of course no method can render human nature objective and impartial. Jews, Catholics, and Protestants will still have their distinctive preferences and prejudices, and there will always be disagreement on fundamental issues. But at least historical criticism provides a forum for rational discussion, where Jews and Christians can explore the reasons that underlie their different theological positions.

Jon D. Levenson challenges the idea that historical criticism can provide common ground for Jewish and Christian interpretation, and argues instead that it is merely neutral territory. Levenson recognizes that historical criticism is not inherently Christian (more specifically Protestant) and that the Christian prejudices of much biblical scholarship are in violation of the method itself. But if historical criticism is

7. See Fish, *Authority of Interpretive Communities*, 305-21.

8. Rendtorff directly makes no such claim, although the ideal of interpreting the Hebrew Bible "from within" might lend itself to that inference.

9. See Collins, "Critical Biblical Theology."

10. The most lucid exposition of the principles of historical criticism remains that of Harvey, *The Historian and the Believer*.

consistently carried out, what is specifically Christian, or Jewish, about it? Against this approach, Murphy argues that a Christian interpretation of the Old Testament does not have to be uniquely or even distinctively Christian. Christian identity has never depended on one specific interpretation of the older Scripture. To be sure, each particular identity—Jewish or Christian—requires continuity with a particular tradition; but the traditions themselves are pluriform, and continuity can be achieved in different ways. Christians do not have to read the Bible as a unified and coherent book, and in fact they seldom do so. From a Christian point of view, then, it is not necessarily problematic to affirm the Hebrew Bible as part of the tradition without finding anything distinctively Christian in it. The issue here depends on the criteria we are willing to accept for Jewish or Christian identity, and there may be less diversity on the Jewish side. If we accept, however, that religious identity is rooted in tradition rather than in the biblical canon, then there is considerably less pressure to find a distinctively Christian, or Jewish, way of reading the Hebrew Scriptures.

It is in this context that Sanders's work on the textual tradition of the Bible is important. The Hebrew Bible is not a univocal entity but exists in textual traditions and manuscripts that were themselves products of communities. For example, the Greek text of Esther deserves serious consideration beside the Hebrew. Sanders's article gives rise to questions about the nature of biblical authority: Is one text more authoritative than another? If so, why? It would seem that an interest in the full history of transmission requires that authority not be invested in any one text but that the whole tradition be regarded as a storehouse of resources from which the modern Jew or Christian can draw.[11] We can affirm *both* Hebrew Bible and Old Testament only if we relativize both, recognizing that each may

11. Compare Sanders's earlier article, "Adaptable for Life," 531-60.

contain much that is of value, while neither is definitive. Equally, if we are to find genuinely common ground in a historical-critical reading of the Bible, this can only be on the understanding that the decisive traditions which give Judaism and Christianity their distinctive identities are to be found elsewhere.

READING RELIGIOUS TEXTS IN COMMUNITY

The discussions of particular texts—the Cain and Abel story, the creation of humanity, the Suffering Servant, and the Song of Songs—show that traditional interpretation is largely an unmined resource that is inherently interesting and can contribute much to the understanding of the text. As James L. Kugel makes clear, historical criticism has been impoverished too often by neglect of the tradition. Biblical studies in the next generation surely will expand the uses of traditional understanding: Christian scholars must improve their use and appreciation of the medieval rabbinic exegetical and grammatical texts; Jewish biblical scholars must learn of the history of interpretation carried out in Christian exegetical traditions.

Traditional interpretation cannot, however, provide the framework for contemporary theology. On the one hand, traditional Christian interpretation is too deeply imbued with the supersessionist view of the Old Testament. On the other hand, traditional methods of interpretation are no longer convincing. Indeed, much of the charm of traditional material lies in its quaintness and remoteness from modern ways of thinking. It may be true that the Old Testament meant more to Christians when they could find the doctrine of the Trinity in Genesis chapter 1, but surely the loss in meaning is preferable in such cases. What we learn from traditional interpretation is not that it contains the so-called true meaning of the text, but

that all interpretation is relative to the concerns, questions, and
presuppositions of the age that produces it.

It is true, however, that there is some asymmetry between
Jewish and Christian attitudes on this point. Modern Jewish
scholars are usually much more comfortable with rabbinic
interpretation than many of their Christian counterparts are
with the church fathers, perhaps because of rabbinic emphases
upon the contextual meaning (פשט) of each text as the
foundation for all later expansive interpretation. At any rate,
the changes wrought by Christian allegory in the meaning of
the biblical text are more apparent to us than the distinctive
emphases of the rabbis. Nonetheless, the rabbis too were guided
by the concerns of their time, and these concerns do not
necessarily coincide with those of the modern age.

Debates on the best answers to these questions continue to
rage: Old, First, Prime—what is the Testament's proper name?
Is a common reading of our Scriptures possible? Desirable? Or
is the cost simply too great, in terms of the loss of religious
traditions implied by historical-critical methodology? This
book, we hope, carries forward the debate, even if it cannot
resolve the basic issues.

Part One

What's in a Name?

The Problem of What We Study

Old Testament/*Tanakh*—Canon and Interpretation

ROLAND E. MURPHY, O. CARM.

Recent developments in biblical theology have made us all aware of the theological potential of the term *canon*. Formerly it was merely dismissed as the list(s) of biblical books. Its history was so prickly that it was left mainly for technical historians to deal with, from the so-called synod of Jamnia to the Council of Trent and beyond. Now, thanks to the "canonical shape" of Brevard Childs and the "canonical criticism" of James A. Sanders, the word has become a hermeneutical key. This rapid canonization of biblical studies leaves us with some questions that go far deeper than book lists or the terminology of Hebrew Bible/*Tanakh* on the one hand and Old Testament/First Testament on the other.[1] I would like to explore some of these issues by stating certain theses and discussing them.

1. "First Testament" is the proposal of James A. Sanders ("First Testament and Second," 47-49), which has been tentatively adopted by the editors of the *Biblical Theology Bulletin*. For the use of the phrase, "Prime Testament," see Lacocque, "The 'Old Testament' in the Protestant Tradition," 120-43, especially 121. Attention may be called here to footnote 1 in the "Notes on the Correct Way to Present Jews and Judaism": "We continue to use the expression Old Testament because it is traditional (cf. already 2 Cor. 3:14) and also because 'old' does not mean 'out of date' or 'outworn.' In any case it is the permanent value of the Old Testament as a source of Christian revelation that is

THE INCONGRUITY OF "HEBREW BIBLE" AND "OLD TESTAMENT"

The Old Testament and the Hebrew Bible are not really the same entities. First of all, although the Protestant Old Testament and the Hebrew Bible are coterminous, this apparent similarity masks a profound difference: the Hebrew Bible is essentially a three-stepped canon, whereas the Old Testament lacks this structure. Even the term *canon* is to be applied cautiously since it betrays a Christian conceptuality that may not do justice to the reality of Jewish tradition, which spoke of books that do or do not soil the hands.[2] This is not the place to enter into the complicated history of the Jewish canon.[3] Suffice it to say that around 100 C.E. there was a clear understanding that the Hebrew Bible had received the contours it presently has, with or without the help of the very problematic "synod" of Jamnia. Outside of what came to be defined as Pharisaic and rabbinic Judaism there may have been a looser practical usage involving the Apocrypha and other books, but we are ill informed about the reality of this. The evidence from Qumran is inconclusive, and the presence of the Apocrypha in later

emphasized here (*Dei Verbum*, 3)"; cf. *Origins* 15/7 (July 4, 1985): 102-7, and the *Osservatore Romano* for June 24, 1985.

Within the New Testament the preferred term for the Jewish Bible is γραφή, in the singular or plural. The use of the phrase "Old Testament" to designate the Bible is first attested in Melito of Sardis (τα τῆς παλαιᾶς διαθῆκης βιβλία), c. 180. This terminology is continued in Clement of Alexandria and Tertullian, and in the canons of the Council of Laodicea in the fourth century which determined that only books of the Old and New Testaments are to be read in the Church. However, if "Old Testament" is not a biblical phrase, it has a biblical basis (cf. the reference to the "reading of the old covenant" in 2 Cor. 3:14, and the use of Jer. 31:31ff. in Heb. 8:8ff.).

2. See the discussion concerning the Song of Songs and Qohelet in Mishnah *Yadayim* 3:5.

3. See especially Sundberg, *Old Testament of the Early Church*; Leiman, *Canon and Masorah*; Barthélemy, *Le canon de l'Ancien Testament*, 9-46.

Christian manuscripts of the Septuagint proves nothing about a different canon in the Diaspora.

It is not for a Christian to analyze the implications for Judaism of a tripartite canon of *Torah*, *Nevi'im*, and *Ketuvim*. Without trying to discern a canon within the canon, I simply point out the fact of the centrality of the Torah in Jewish belief and practice.[4] A *canon within the canon* is Christian terminology and is born out of Christian theology, especially out of the analysis of the Pauline Epistles. I would remark in passing that this Christian concept, as it is practiced, does not do justice to the richness of the biblical word.[5]

The point to be emphasized is that the Old Testament is a considerably less structured compilation than the Hebrew Bible. A traditional division into historical, prophetic, and poetical books tells one very little about them. One reason why Childs's canonical approach to the Hebrew Bible is so interesting is his resolute adherence to the tripartite structure of Law, Prophets, and Writings.[6] His emphasis is upon shape, not process: specifically, the canonical shape of the individual books of the Hebrew Bible in its entirety, as this was fixed by the Jewish

4. On this point many Jewish authors may be cited. See, for example, Cohen, "Record and Revelation," 147-71, especially 150: "Although the entire *Tanakh* is regarded as holy, its first section, the *Torah*, is held as the holiest and the most fundamental text of Judaism's sacred tradition."

5. Cf. the remarks of R. E. Brown in *The New Jerome Biblical Commentary*, edited by R. E. Brown et al. (Englewood Cliffs, N. J.: Prentice-Hall, 1990), 67: 92-97.

6. See Brevard Childs, *Introduction to the Old Testament*. This view of Childs is to be distinguished from the "canonical criticism" of James A. Sanders. The latter is interested in the reconstruction of the *process* of the formation of the Hebrew Bible, especially from the Exile on. He draws out hermeneutical implications from the process itself, from the questions that the community presumably asked itself as it went about collecting and editing its national legacy. This process has hermeneutical implications for today's reader of the Bible. We are to be guided somehow by the process that we can discern. Cf. Sanders, *From Sacred Story to Sacred Text*, with references to his earlier studies.

community of about 100 C.E. He zeroes in on this state as the final form or direction that the Jewish community gave to the Bible, and it becomes a hermeneutical principle for understanding the biblical message. Biblical meaning is not to be derived from a hypothetical source (for example, Yahwist or Elohist) in the Pentateuch as reconstructed by modern scholarship. One is to read the Pentateuch from the point of view of its final canonical shape, the intention given to it by the Jewish tradition that formed the Torah. Childs is faulted by many critics.[7] While his approach does yield a valid meaning, this is not the only one; several levels of meaning must be recognized in the Bible. Moreover, his approach to the Scriptures prescinds, as much as a Christian interpreter can manage, from the fact that the Hebrew Bible is given a new canonical shape by reason of its being included with a New Testament in a canon that is broader than that of Jewish tradition. Nonetheless, he underscores a dimension of biblical interpretation that has been practically neglected by Christians: the tripartite division of the Hebrew Bible has important and valid insights to offer the Christian who is ready to evaluate the Hebrew Bible on its own terms.[8]

A second aspect of the dissimilarity between the Hebrew Bible and the Old Testament concerns the addition of the Apocrypha, in the tradition of the early Church and Roman Catholicism, surely not a negligible difference. It has been stated by G. E. Wright that the "marginal" books are not the basis for

---

7. See the critique in *Journal for the Study of the Old Testament* 16 (1980): 2-60; see also the detailed treatment in Barr, *Holy Scripture*, 130-71.

8. This point can be illustrated by the various studies of such Jewish scholars as Moshe Greenberg, Nahum Sarna, and Jon D. Levenson. I shall argue later that a Christian reading of the Old Testament can learn much from them, while still remaining faithful to itself.

"any central issue for faith or life."[9] But theological discussion is not the issue; the point is one of fact as to the authenticity of a given book as the word of God for the community of faith. Moreover, evaluating a book for its pertinence to central issues of theology is a kind of reductionism. The simple fact is that the community is dependent upon the word, which in turn must somehow be defined or delimited. Since the community has a long life, various books—despite intermittent or lengthy periods of obscurity—can eventually become important in the life of the community and certainly in the lives of individuals who accept them as canonical and holy. What may be marginal to one individual or historical period may be central to another.

As is well known, the working canon of the early Church and of the Roman Catholic church included the Apocrypha. The influence of Augustine, reflecting a broader base and contrary to Jerome and his *veritas hebraica*, prevailed until the Reformation. The implication is this: while the Old Testament is a legacy from the Jewish community, its extent (as well as its configuration) was determined early on by the Church on its own authority.

It will be helpful to give an example of how the addition of the Apocrypha to the canon affects interpretation. In the Hebrew Bible, three wisdom books are to be found among the Writings: Proverbs, Job, and Ecclesiastes (Qohelet). Sirach and the Wisdom of Solomon are added to these in the Old Testament of the Catholic tradition. What is the difference created by the two Apocrypha? A new interpretive context is created. One cannot be satisfied with a common verdict found among *Alttestamentler* to the effect that wisdom became bankrupt with the appearance of Qohelet, or even worse, that

9. Wright, *Old Testament and Theology*, 168. The same view is expressed frequently by James Barr (for example, *The Bible and the Modern World*, 154; *Holy Scripture*, 41-42).

Qohelet is to be marginalized within the Bible, perhaps to be treated merely as a point of view that was calling for the new vision of Christianity. Such downplaying of this book is uncalled for.

What light is shed on Qohelet by Ben Sira and the Wisdom of Solomon, by contextualizing the work within the wisdom tradition? First, it seems obvious that wisdom is not bankrupt in the eyes of Sirach and the Diaspora author of Wisdom. They both continue the wisdom tradition. While they do not engage in direct dialogue with Ecclesiastes, they relativize his message about the vanity of life by their own positive evaluation of wisdom. The basic contention of Qohelet was that the vanity of life flowed from human inability to know the "work of God" (Eccles. 3:11; 8:17; 11:5). Sirach and Wisdom do not penetrate this mystery, but they do wrestle with it in an ongoing fashion. Second, an important theological development takes place. Whatever be the correct evaluation of the eschatology in the Greek form of Sirach, there is no doubt about the doctrine concerning the next life in the Wisdom of Solomon. What is not sufficiently appreciated is the typically biblical way by which the author of Wisdom arrives at the doctrine of immortality. It is not sought in the nature of the soul (or even in the resurrection of the body) but in a relationship with the Lord: "Righteousness is undying" (Wisd. of Sol. 1:15). The Greek doctrine of the natural immortality of the soul may well have been known to the author, but that is not the way he expresses immortality. He is much more in the thought pattern of Ps. 73:23ff.: "With you I shall always be . . . . Though my flesh and my heart waste away, God is the rock of my heart and my portion forever."

Our treatment of the extent of the canon would be incomplete if two implicit problems were to go unmentioned. First, there is the biblical text itself. Textual criticism has made it difficult in many cases to fasten securely on one version of the text of a given book. I refer, for example, to the books of Job and Jeremiah, or Proverbs and Sirach, where the Greek form (Septuagint) has significant departures from the Massoretic text. Modern discoveries show clearly that the pre-Massoretic Hebrew text was not as uniform as was once thought. Which text is to be followed? Can we speak of a canonical text? Sirach is a case in point, insofar as we possess only about two-thirds of the Hebrew in which it was originally written, and the Greek form has wide-ranging departures. My own inclination is to settle for an inspired book, and let the textual form of the book be determined by the art of textual criticism, however faulty and uncertain it may be in given instances.[10]

The question is aggravated by the role that the Greek translation(s) played in the history of the Church. Many theologians have claimed that the Septuagint is in fact an inspired translation of the Bible. This is not because any credence is to be given to the legend surrounding the translation of the Seventy. The theological argument is that the Septuagint was the Bible of the early Church and is most often referred to in the New Testament. This view of Augustine has been taken up in modern times by French exegetes, among them such experts in textual criticism as Dominique Barthélemy.[11] I would grant that the Septuagint played a providential role in the hellenizing of the Hebrew Bible for Christians, but it is a translation and remains one. Its authority

10. I agree with the lengthy discussion of Sirach by Hartman, "Sirach in Hebrew and in Greek," 443-51, that one can speak only of an inspired book, not an inspired text. For a differing point of view, see Kearns, "Ecclesiasticus," who favors "the text of Sirach as it has been read in the Christian Church from the beginning." Gilbert argues that both text types, the shorter and the longer, are canonical and inspired (cf. Gilbert, "L'Ecclésiastique," 233-50). See also the essays by James A. Sanders and Eugene Ulrich in this volume.

11. See Barthélemy, *Etudes d'histoire du texte*, 110-39, with references to other exegetes, such as Benoit.

comes from its proper reflection of a Hebrew (or in some cases Aramaic) original. It is up to the practitioners of textual criticism to establish the original form as critically as possible, even if in many instances no certainty can be arrived at. That, too, seems part of providence: the communities of faith live without the original autographs or even copies close in time that would give such certainty. They live with many uncertainties, among them the precise form of the text of the word of God.

The second issue that deserves mention in this context is the growth of the Old Testament, especially the Septuagint, in the form of glosses and additions. Are these truly part of the Bible, and not merely incidental reflections on the part of the community of faith? The analogous problem in the New Testament is the unquestionable addition to the Gospel of John about the woman taken in adultery (John 7:53-8:11). Whether one is speaking of a minute gloss or a large portion, it is impossible to determine any cutoff point. I think the Catholic practice is to rely on the biblical character of substantial portions that would have been read in the Bible transmitted to the community (the *vetus et vulgata editio*, as the Council of Trent put it). But this is not an absolute criterion.

THE NEW TESTAMENT AS CONTEXT FOR THE OLD TESTAMENT

For the Christian, the Old Testament is affected by its inclusion in a broader canon that includes the New Testament. What are the implications of this? One might begin by considering three of the premises that stand behind the appropriation of the Old Testament: the Jewishness of Jesus; his (and the Christian's) understanding of the God of the Old Testament as Jesus' Father; the fact that the Old Testament was the only Bible of the primitive Church.

First, the Jewishness of Jesus means more than simply the need for a Christian to know the Old Testament in order to understand Jesus or his message. He himself was nourished by the Law and the Prophets according to the lights of his time and his own interpretive genius. He was not an exegete, and he laid down no rules for hermeneutics. But the very fact that he grappled with the Bible suffices to authorize a Christian to adopt the Bible of Jesus as his or her own. This is part of what *imitatio Christi* means. The Christ, and the Christian, is inconceivable without roots in Jesus' Bible.

Second, in the Christian view, this Bible witnesses to the revelation of the God and Father of Jesus Christ. The Old Testament contains not only the roots of Christian identity, but also the precious witness to the ongoing revelation of God which came to a climax in Christ. Thus Heb. 1:1-2—"In times past God spoke in fragmentary and varied ways to our fathers through the prophets; in this, the final age, he has spoken to us through his Son"—has implications for a Christian understanding of the Old Testament *on its terms*: What did God say to the fathers?

Third, the Old Testament was the only Bible of the primitive Church; that is, the Christian had recourse to it to explain Christ. This point has been made well by James Barr.[12] Jesus was the person to be understood. The Old Testament was not a text to be subjected to exegesis or explained in all the levels of its meaning. Christ was the new event which called for understanding. The New Testament style of exegesis, or what may be called the christocentric interpretation of the Old Testament, is a particular line into the riches of the Old Testament, but it is not the only one, as we shall see. It is a phenomenon that is different from our (later) hermeneutical

12. Barr, *Old and New in Interpretation*, 139-41.

approach to a body of literature. In other words, the role of the Old Testament in nourishing the faith of the Christian *after Christ* is different from the one it had in explaining Christ. With the necessity of history, the Christian family has become involved in an hermeneutical analysis of the Old Testament. This is a valid and exciting enterprise that opens up more avenues into the text than the christological. Karl Rahner associates the inspired character of the Bible with the fact that it was a constitutive element of the primitive Church.[13] The Bible thus became a kind of norm for the Church to judge herself against throughout history. This norm is not to be conceived as apart from the ongoing tradition which interprets it. The peculiar tilt of Catholicism to the role of tradition and the consensus of the community delivers it from a slavery to biblical literalism and opens it to a development which is analogous both to the phenomenon of inner-biblical interpretation so well described by Michael Fishbane,[14] and perhaps to the phenomenon of the oral Law of Jewish tradition.

At this point an important conclusion can be drawn. There is no one univocal Christian understanding (for example, christological) of the Old Testament. The historical fact that various Christian scholars (including Walther Eichrodt, Gerhard von Rad, and others) have attempted to relate Old Testament and New Testament in various ways and with varying degrees of success is a witness to this. I am not interested in judging their efforts, but simply in recognizing the various directions that, as history shows, have been taken by Christian scholars. The attempt is certainly not new; it goes back

---

13. Rahner, *Inspiration in the Bible.*
14. Fishbane, *Biblical Interpretation in Ancient Israel.*

to the early Church, and it is still with us.[15] In the course of the history of interpretation one finds typology, allegory, fuller sense, and all kinds of hermeneutical ploys that attempt to interpret the Old Testament in the light of the New. This is a perfectly valid enterprise and it should be judged by its successes and failures. But a Christian interpretation of the Old Testament should not be locked into a narrow track (for example, christological interpretation), nor should it be dominated by the question of the relationship between the Testaments. An interpretation can be Christian, not because it is done by a Christian, but because it touches a level of meaning that has significance on its own terms (within the Hebrew Bible), and also in the light of the context of both Testaments. I would not deny that there are continuities and discontinuities in such a reading. A vision of faith is necessary to affirm continuities. But the discontinuities are also very important, and one may not jettison them in favor of continuities. They are there to challenge the Christian reader, and I shall return to this question of tensions within the Bible.

But I am not in agreement with those who highlight simple discontinuities. Antonius Gunneweg writes, "While the religion of the Old Testament may not come into the category of an alien religion, it is still pre-Christian and, without Christ, un-Christian." He asks dramatically, "Is the God who marched before Joshua and the Israelites in their bloody battles and commanded them to exterminate the enemy the God of Jesus Christ?"[16] To that I would reply in the affirmative, stressing the limitations both of images and of any human perception of God, inside or outside the Bible. The limitations of the biblical

15. The state of the question has hardly changed since my summary in Murphy, "The Relationship Between the Testaments," 349-59; see also Murphy, "Christian Understanding," 321-32.
16. Cf. Gunneweg, *Understanding the Old Testament*, 220-23.

word are not easily recognized by those who live by *sola scriptura*. Moreover, Gunneweg makes the New Testament the criterion of the canonicity of the Old Testament, that is, Christian beliefs are to determine canonicity: "It is impossible to make any decision on the Christian canon which can be applied generally to all its parts." This is to confuse interpretation with canonicity. Interpretation cannot create or rule on a canon which has been fixed by the authority of the community of faith, any more than Judaism can eliminate a book of the Hebrew Bible because it is inconvenient to standards fixed by later interpretation. It is ironic that a Protestant theology, expressly committed to the biblical word, should make an interpretation of the New Testament the arbiter of the canonical status of an earlier part of the Bible.

In this connection, Jon D. Levenson quotes with approval the following statement of Gunneweg: "But it is impossible to give a Christian interpretation of something that is not Christian; Christian interpretation of something that is not Christian is pseudo-interpretation." Levenson characterizes this as a devastating "judgment on two millennia of biblical studies in a distinctively Christian mode."[17] Not so. Gunneweg is mistaken. Levenson sees in the efforts of von Rad and other *Alttestamentler* the "sin of anachronism," and he regards the phrase "Old Testament" as an "a-historical, or anachronistic term." This depends on definitions. It is a historical term that grew up out of the self-understanding of the Christian community. It may be anachronistic insofar as it reflects an understanding which the people of the Hebrew Bible never had of themselves, but one has to appreciate the vantage points of time and of religious perspective.

---

17. Levenson, "Hebrew Bible, the Old Testament, and Historical Criticism," 48-49; see also 28 and 50.

I have mentioned discontinuities between the Testaments. The relationships can be seen as dialectical. That is to say, some aspects of the Old Testament in their very strangeness and difference are particularly pertinent to a Christian because they serve as a necessary ballast to emphases in the New Testament and in Christian life. A case in point is the highly individualized eschatology to be found in Paul ("our citizenship is in heaven," Phil. 3:20; cf. Col. 3:1-3), and which can be appropriated in too facile a manner by Christians. The Old Testament emphasis on this world (often misunderstood as materialistic), and the relationship of the individual to the Lord in the here and now correct Christian exaggeration. I am not demeaning the Old Testament in this, as if I were merely making do with it. I am praising it and I am grateful for it. Christians need experience of Jewish faith. Perhaps a Jew standing in the Pharisaic tradition, which also accepts an individualized eschatology in the world to come, also feels the need of this Old Testament emphasis. Tensions exist between the Testaments, and within each individual Testament. These are precious indications of the complexity of divine revelation and of human response.

TOWARD BIBLICAL THEOLOGY

I would like to apply the preceding remarks to some issues of biblical theology.

Until very recently, Old Testament theology was a Christian, not a Jewish preserve. This may have been due to the particular Jewish tradition of the oral Torah, to the strong role that tradition plays in molding the Jewish view of life. Jewish theology can be said to resemble dogmatic or systematic theology in that it is a theology based on the Bible. Now the Jewish scholar, Moshe Goshen-Gottstein, has gently taken to task the academic guild for its jejune and aseptic treatment of the Bible on an allegedly objective plane (historical-critical methodology), and he indicated that the time had come to discuss theological issues at such meetings as the International Organization for the Study of the Old Testament.[18]

On the other hand, but perhaps not in serious disagreement with Goshen-Gottstein, Levenson has written an article, "Why Jews Are Not Interested in Biblical Theology."[19] The reasons he gives are familiar: the field has been a Protestant preoccupation, and it is not free from Christian presuppositions about Torah. Levenson also rejects the approach of historical criticism because of its limitations (if not its distortions), in favor of a synchronic approach (or the "literary simultaneity of Scripture") that is congenial to the Jewish tradition.[20] If I understand him correctly, his concern is systematic theology, not merely biblical theology, for ultimately the biblical text is unabashedly understood in the framework of Judaism, and the tradition of the oral Torah.[21]

---

18. Cf. Goshen-Gottstein, "Christianity, Judaism and Modern Bible Study," 69-88. He has long taught a course in *Tanakh* theology, and he has revealed something of the shape it takes; see his "*Tanakh* Theology," 617-44. See also Tsevat, "Theology of the Old Testament," 33-50, with a response from B. W. Anderson, 51-59.

19. See Neusner, Levine, and Frerichs, *Judaic Perspectives on Ancient Israel*, 281-307.

20. Cf. Levenson, "Eighth Principle of Judaism," 205-25.

21. The position of the Hebrew Scriptures within Judaism is clearly and forcefully stated by Neusner in *Judaism and Scripture*, xi: "While the world at large treats Judaism as 'the religion of the Old Testament,' the fact is otherwise. Judaism inherits and makes the Hebrew Scriptures its own, just as does Christianity. But just as Christianity rereads the entire heritage of ancient Israel in light of 'the resurrection of Jesus Christ,' so Judaism understands the Hebrew Scriptures as only one part, the written one, of 'the one whole Torah of Moses, our rabbi.' Ancient Israel no more testified to the oral Torah, now written down in the Mishnah and later rabbinic writings, than it did to Jesus as the Christ. . . . Since the Judaism at hand first reached literary expression in the Mishnah, a document in which Scripture plays a subordinate role, the founders of that Judaism clearly make no pretense at tying up to scriptural prooftexts or at expressing in the form of scriptural commentary the main ideas they wished

Similarly, Rolf Rendtorff has recently put the question quite sharply, "Must 'biblical theology' be *Christian* theology?"[22] One answer, in effect, swallows up the Old Testament into the New Testament, and does not take it on its own terms. Another approach makes it into a so-called history of religion. Rendtorff's preference is to "examine the theology of the Hebrew Bible, independently of any later developments, whether Christian or Jewish." This means discovering the message of the biblical authors, that is, the "final authors, or redactors, or editor, those who are responsible for the final edition as it has come down to us. We *must* do this because these are the only texts we have." It would appear that for Rendtorff, as for Childs, the prehistory of the text (for example, the theology of the Yahwist) is not the concern of biblical theology. Where is one to begin? He starts with creation, but in the context of sin and promise. This holistic reading of Genesis, according to Rendtorff, yields the same structure as in the Sinai story: threat and covenant. It is perhaps unfair to judge Rendtorff by an article that was designedly popular and not meant to convey his full thought on the topic. But I doubt that his reading of Genesis is holistic enough. It is a systematization of Genesis and Sinai that is honorable, but limited; and it leaves other areas of the Old Testament untouched. Its real strength is that it takes the Old Testament on its own terms.

I would like to conclude by giving an answer to Rendtorff's question—"Must 'biblical theology' be *Christian* theology?" The answer is no, and it is best understood in the light of the following definition of terms. One speaks of Old Testament (or

---

to set out. Accordingly, Judaism only asymmetrically rests upon the foundations of the Hebrew Scriptures, and Judaism is not alone or mainly 'the religion of the Old Testament.'"

22. See Rendtorff, "'Biblical Theology,'" 40-43. See also Rendtorff, "'Covenant.'"

Tanakh) theology, New Testament theology, and a biblical theology that also involves the relationship between the two Testaments. The theology of any one Testament can be described as the systematization in biblical categories of the understanding of God, humans, and creation. A theology *based upon* a given Testament is at least one step removed from that.

Can one speak of a theology of the Old Testament? I do not think it is possible to systematize *one* theology for the whole, to establish a conceptual unity to the Old Testament, that is, to find its center, or to organize the biblical data under one or more overarching concepts.[23] The Bible is simply too varied and rich for any logical systematization of its theology. This does not mean abandoning biblical theology, but recognizing its selective, incomplete character, while at the same time opening the Bible to more detailed, if less unified, analysis. The great achievements of Eichrodt, von Rad, and others have been criticized from several points of view, by both Christian and Jewish scholars. But their magnificent failures have taught almost everyone to be wary of oversystematization. The Old Testament provides several theologies, and it should be heard in its pluralism. It may be objected that this amounts to fragmentation of the biblical message, but this understanding preserves one from the danger of a subjective selectivity. It simply attempts to preserve the individuality and uniqueness of theological ideas in the Bible as opposed to a process of homogenization. The Bible was not written for the sake of theology.

---

23. The literature on the unity and the center of the Bible is voluminous. Convenient summaries can be found in Reventlow, *Problems of Old Testament Theology*. I have expressed my views in a dialogue with Rolf Knierim (see Knierim, "Task of Old Testament Theology"; and Murphy, "Response").

A necessary ingredient in biblical theology is the much maligned historical-critical methodology.[24] But this important tool, the product of Deism and the Enlightenment, is not to be blamed for what it cannot deliver, a complete meaning of the biblical word. What it does, it does well. It reaches, in the only way presently available to us, into the historicity of the text and its affirmations. Of course it has its presuppositions and limitations, but nothing else is available to replace it.

It may be asked, How does biblical *theology* (of either Testament) differ from a *history* of Israelite/Christian religion? I think that the prime difference is the basic presupposition that the believing theologian accepts the witness of the Testament to a transcendent Lord, whereas the pure historian regards the Bible as simply a historical document, interpreted with empathy no doubt, but without such commitment. For the biblical theologian, the issue is the truth and validity of the biblical messages. Other factors also affect the way in which interpretation takes place: To what extent does one recognize limitations on the biblical word? (An obvious example would be the varying positions on the truth of the Bible.) To what extent does a Christian or Judaic tradition mold one's interpretation of a text? (An obvious example would be the differences in the evaluation of Torah.) As an attempt to sensitize students to their presuppositions in an Old Testament theology course, I ask them to list and comment on certain Old Testament ideas which as much as possible need *not* be filtered through New Testament glasses—ideas that are therefore genuinely biblical and attested clearly and magnificently in the Old Testament. This approach is guided by historical-critical

24. Not all would agree with the use of this method. Cf. Levenson, "Hebrew Bible, the Old Testament, and Historical Criticism," 19-59. A different position is adopted by Sperling, "Judaism and Modern Biblical Research," 19-44. See also Fitzmyer, "Historical Criticism," 244-59.

methodology. It is instructive to question the students
concerning the basis of their selection, and to inquire why
certain data were omitted (one invariably thinks of Old
Testament cult and Torah). I have found this an instructive
way to open up the riches of the Old Testament to a twentieth-
century Christian, and to create an awareness of what
interpretation means. No interpreter can dispense with his or
her presuppositions; they are inevitably at work. But if they are
openly recognized, a great deal of ecumenical harmony and
mutual understanding can be achieved.

My point can be exemplified by the Book of Psalms. This has
long been considered as a prayerbook of the Christian
community, in part because of its extensive use in the liturgy.
By and large, the traditional patristic understanding has been
clearly christocentric.[25] This christological position is at a
disadvantage: it is not the obvious sense; more importantly it
closes in the meaning—or simply closes it off. I do not dispute
the right of a Christian to carry an understanding forward to a
christological framework, but neither do I deem this a *necessary*
step for an interpretation to be Christian. In the matter of
prayer, freedom to move with the word is perhaps the most
fundamental law; no one prayer style can really be prescribed.
In the case of the Psalms, historical-critical scholarship has
enriched our understanding of them, despite the uncertainties
of *Sitz im Leben* and other niceties. The language, in its many
allusions to the world of myth, has begun to come clear for the
modern reader who makes an effort to understand it. The
enormous range of the description of the human condition
before God is perhaps the chief reason why the Psalms exercise
such fascination, and almost of themselves overcome
hermeneutical barriers. They have a general open-ended

25. Cf. Fischer, *Die Psalmen als Stimme.*

character that registers in the experience of the modern reader, whether Christian or Jewish.[26]

Another illustration is the Song of Songs and the history of its interpretation. In a reverse way it is a good example of the value of the approach of historical criticism. It is a striking fact that both Jewish and Christian interpretation, as far back as we can go, fixed on a meaning that is not the obvious one of the text. The partners in the Song were judged to be not sexual human beings, but God and God's People. In the Jewish view the relationship between the Lord and Israel was described, as the Targum makes clear. For the Christian, as exemplified by Origen and countless later interpreters who followed in his footsteps, this was applied to the relationship between Christ and the Church or the individual soul. I would not say that these interpretations are invalid. But they *are* one-sided. They do not recognize the human sexual dimension which is inherent in the Song. It is due primarily to historical criticism that one can justify the validity of this dimension, which the traditional interpretation all but snuffed out.[27]

Perhaps these considerations about Old Testament/Hebrew Bible indicate that we all have something to learn from each other in the matter of interpreting Old Testament/Hebrew Bible. Speaking as a Catholic, I can only say that I have learned much from my Protestant and Jewish colleagues.

26. Cf. Murphy, *Psalms, Job*; and Miller, *Interpreting the Psalms*.
27. One of the best studies of Song of Songs is Fox, *Song of Songs*.

The New Covenant, Jesus, and Canonization

JOSEPHINE MASSYNGBAERDE FORD

Roland E. Murphy, O. Carm., raises three issues for productive work on the Hebrew Bible. These are, first, the use of the terms "Prime Covenant" or Testament in contrast to the "New Covenant" or Testament; second, the Jewishness of Jesus and Paul; and third, the relationship between the process of so-called canonization (or, preferably, the collection of Sacred Writings) and the worshipping community.

NEW COVENANT

I begin with an obvious and simple statement but one that has, I think, been overlooked. In the opening three-quarters of the first century C.E. (to c. 68, 70, or 74),[1] we have documentary evidence for two Jewish communities, both of which claimed to be communities of the New Covenant. The first community is that of the Qumran covenanters. They designated themselves

---

1. These years mark the destruction of the Qumran settlement, the fall of Jerusalem, and the conquest of Masada respectively.

specifically in the Damascus Rule as people who had entered
the New Covenant (באי הברית החדשה):[2]

- "to observe the Sabbath day according to its exact tenor,
  and the feasts, and the Day of Fasting according to the
  [commands] of those who have entered the New
  Covenant in the land of Damascus" (CD 6:19)
- "all the men who entered the New Covenant in the land
  of Damascus" (CD 8:21)
- "similarly, none of all those men who have entered the
  New Covenant but have turned back and betrayed (it) in
  the land of Damascus" (CD 19:33-34)
- "and for having despised the covenant and the Pact which
  they made in the land of Damascus, which is the New
  Covenant" (CD 20:12)

Of these references, none appears to be in the immediate
context of Jer. 31:31. The designation of "old" or "prime"
Testament is not found; but a similar phrase, "the covenant of
the ancestors," (ברית ראשנים) occurs, for example, in CD 1:4 ("But
remembering the Covenant of the ancestors, he left a remnant
to Israel") and CD 3:10 ("And because of this the first to enter
the Covenant of the ancestors [were rendered guilty] and were
delivered up to the sword").

The second community of the New Covenant is that of the
Jewish-Christian community. The specific phrases (ἡ καινή
διαθήκη or διαθήκη νέα) occur in these contexts:

- "the New Covenant in my blood" (Luke 22:20)
- "this cup is the new covenant in my blood" (1 Cor. 11:25)
- "who made us qualified ministers of a new covenant, a
  covenant not of written law but of spirit" (2 Cor. 3:6)

---

2. Lohse, *Die Texte aus Qumran*; English translation, Dupont-Sommer,
Essene Writings from Qumran.

- "therefore he is the mediator of a new covenant, so that those who are called may receive the promised eternal inheritance, since a death has occurred which redeems them from the transgressions under the first covenant" (Heb. 9:15)
- "Jesus, the mediator of a new covenant" (Heb. 12:24)

The designation for the first covenant, by contrast, is "old covenant" (τῆς παλαιᾶς διαθήκης, 2 Cor. 3:14, cf. also Heb. 9:1).

Both communities may be said to be actively engaged in the *process* of canonization or gathering together Sacred Scriptures. Observe the following affinities between those at Qumran and the early Christians:

- Neither community had a standard Hebrew (or Greek) text.
- They both had an open-ended canon.[3] For example, those at Qumran seemed to regard the Temple Scroll[4] as inspired; it is delivered in the first person singular as if God *per se* were speaking.
- Both communities seem to have seen the notion of canon as adaptable, pluralistic, and multivalent.[5]
- Both interpreted Scripture in the light of contemporary events (which they saw as the *magnalia dei*) and both, at times, used a fusion of scriptural texts when expounding their teaching (e.g. 11 Q Melch. and Luke 4:16-18): but the one emphasized, although not exclusively, *ethos* over *mythos* and the other *mythos* over *ethos*; both had an inspired prophet-teacher and involved "lay people" in the study of the sacred text. See, for example, 1 QS 6:6-8: "And in the place where the ten are, let there not lack a

3. Cf. Blenkinsopp, "Tanakh and the New Testament," 96.
4. Maier, *Templerolle vom Toten Meer*.
5. Sanders, *Canon and Community*, 24; and Blenkinsopp, "Tanakh and the New Testament," 98.

man who studies the Law night and day, continually, concerning the duties of each towards the other."

- Both were critical of the priesthood in Jerusalem: one departed from her and retreated to the desert; the other stayed in the city.
- The destiny of both communities was dramatically affected by the First Jewish-Roman war (66-74 C.E.).
- Both communities felt free to compose their own Scriptures over and above what we now call the Hebrew Bible.
- For both, Wisdom was not bankrupt. The Christian community was influenced by the Greek form of Sirach and Wisdom of Solomon and saw in Jesus the persecuted Righteous One of Wisdom of Solomon chapter 2 and his exaltation in his resurrection (cf. Acts 3:14). The Qumran community saw themselves as the suffering righteous ones who "atoned for the Land" (1 QS 8:3), but in the published documents there is no clear allusion to resurrection.[6] However, the people at Qumran certainly looked forward to an eternal reward and everlasting bliss: "And as for the Visitation of all who walk in this (Spirit), it consists of healing and abundance of bliss, with length of days and fruitfulness, and all blessings without end, and eternal joy in perpetual life, and the glorious crown and garment of honor in everlasting light" (1 QS 4:6-8).

Thus among the Qumran covenanters and within the early Christian community the concept of former/new covenant is found, the covenant members commit themselves to a fulfillment of the Mosaic covenant in a new way, and they see God giving continuous revelation to them.

6. See Duhaime, "La doctrine des Esséniens," 99-121.

PAUL AND THE TORAH

Murphy has mentioned that the Jewishness of Jesus provides a strong link with the Jewish religion. Many Jews could be comfortable with Jesus' approach to the Torah which was so close in many aspects to that of Hillel the Pharisee.[7] It is Paul, however, who would seem to be a stumbling block to our Jewish brothers and sisters. Paul is a good illustration of Murphy's point that *after* Christ (Jesus), Christian exegesis changes. This change is certainly seen in Paul, in contrast, for example, to the Matthean community which saw the fulfillment of the Torah in Jesus and placed upon his lips the statement that not "one jot or tittle" would be abrogated (Matt. 5:17-20).

I should agree that there is a "shift in the dominant mode of perceiving" the Torah in Paul.[8] I agree with James A. Sanders that Paul addressed not only the *ethos* of the Torah but the *mythos* which he saw fulfilled in Christ who for him was the *telos* of the Law.[9] But I am also intrigued by the theory of the Orthodox Jewish scholar Michael Wyschogrod, to whom Sanders gives considerable space.[10] It is Wyschogrod's contention that Paul remained an Orthodox Jew. For Paul, Jesus had taken on the curse of the Law which the *gentiles* incurred for their disobedience, that is, his death annulled *for them* the curses listed in Deuteronomy chapter 28 (cf. Gal. 3:13). Thus he averted God's threat of just judgment against them, not against his Jewish brothers and sisters. The curse is annulled and the

---

7. An old but attractive booklet is still illustrative of this point: Glatzer, *Hillel the Elder.*

8. Hanson, "Biblical Interpretation," 33-34.

9. Sanders, *From Sacred Story to Sacred Text*, 121.

10. I have not been able to discover whether the paper to which Sanders refers has been published.

gentiles participate in a renewed Israel;[11] but like the resident alien (גר תושב), they are obliged to keep only the Noachic commandments (cf. Acts 15:20, 29). The early Jewish Christians continued to worship in the Temple, and Paul took upon himself supererogatory works, such as the Nazirite vow at Cenchrae (Acts 18:18) and the observation of the Jewish festivals (cf. 1 Cor. 16:8). It is interesting also to note that Luke presents Paul as circumcising Timothy immediately after the Council of Jerusalem (Acts 16:1-3). But the fact remains that Paul taught in the Greco-Roman world where purity laws may not have been so important because people were not frequenting the Temple services. Further, from the point of Biblical canon, the converts would perhaps be more accustomed to reading or hearing the Septuagint rather than the Massoretic text.[12] Thus he would be seen as less Orthodox than Jesus.

Over and above Wyschogrod's theory, Sanders speaks of the scholarly tendency to overemphasize the *halakhah* when discussing Paul. But normative Judaism is always "a balance between the two."[13] For Sanders, Paul

> found it necessary to emphasize the Torah as the story of divine election and redemption, in the eschatological conviction that God's recent work in Christ had made that election and that redemption available to all humankind, while at the same time to emphasize those specific stipulations that seemed to present stumbling blocks to carrying out the mandate of God's righteous acts that had found their culmination, goal, and climax in God's eschatological act in Christ. The combination of Torah story and eschaton was adaptable for life wherever it was told to the extent that that story was emphasized and the laws seen as dynamically or spiritually enforced (2 Cor. 3:4-6).[14]

11. Cf. Blenkinsopp, "Tanakh and the New Testament," 99.
12. Cf. Kravitz, "A Jewish Reading," 75-95.
13. Sanders, *From Sacred Story to Sacred Text*, 121.
14. Sanders, *From Sacred Story to Sacred Text*, 121.

Worship and Inspired Writings

The "germ of the formation of the canon is found in the credo."[15] We may add that a credo would be recited and repeated on cultic occasions, thus becoming not the prerogative of the priests or leaders, but of the entire people. This is especially so in the recital of the *haggadah* at the Passover meal, which reverted to being a family celebration after the Fall of the Temple. The reading of the Pentateuch and the Prophets in the synagogue service and the recital of the Targumim also brought the canonical process to the community: later further discussion might have taken place in the study house (בית המדרש). Thus the Torah, in the sense of the *magnalia dei*, was celebrated by the whole community perhaps not only in the formal lections but also in prayer, hymn, commentary, and discussion. This formed the process of canonization within both the Jewish and Christian communities.

Paul and Luke in Acts (insofar as Acts is historical) attest to this process as, for example, is seen from Paul's guidelines about worship in 1 Cor. 14:26-33: "When you assemble, one has a psalm, another has an instruction to give, still another a revelation to share, one speaks in a tongue, another interprets . . . ."

This charismatic worship was apparently celebrated on the same occasion at the Lord's Supper which commemorated the *magnalia dei* in Christ and which handed down the concept of the new covenant in Jesus's blood at the Eucharistic celebration.[16] Thus one finds within Christian worship the growth of the deposit of faith and the collecting of sacred materials through the mediation of both men and women in the public assembly (1 Corinthians chapter 11). The process of canonization might also be seen obliquely in the cultic hymns

---

15. Sanders, *From Sacred Story to Sacred Text*, 14.
16. Sanders, *From Sacred Story to Sacred Text*, 67-70.

of the Christians, notably Phil. 2:5-11 and Col. 1:15-18. But there must have been many others which are no longer extant. I am not sure about Murphy's reference to the Psalms as the prayer of the primitive Church. This does not seem to have obtained until about the fourth century, although Paul does mention "psalm" in 1 Cor. 14:26. So the process of New Testament canon as, indeed, recognized by the form critics, arose in the cultic and didactic milieu of the Christian community. Thus canon is not a list of books (an inverted Index!) but the expression of the faith of the people of God, and these people were both Jewish and pagan Christians. But André Lacocque's point needs to be born in mind:

> The Prime Testament, as the document, was preceded and followed, surrounded, by the community of Israel. *Per contra* the New Testament precedes the Church and presides to its constitution. The prophets of old were within their people's fold and are unthinkable without it.[17]

Even after the formation of the list of canonical books (which was certainly not completed before the fourth century) there was no uniformity among the early Christians.[18] The Eastern church retained the deuterocanonical books, and the Ethiopian church had the most extensive canon.[19]

In one sense, one can say that the Christians' defense of their Jewish heritage is found in their response to Marcion for his anti-Semitic attempt to expunge the Old Testament from the sacred books of the Christians. This was a stimulus to the formation of canon in the sense of a list of books and thus protected the Hebrew Bible.

17. Lacocque, "'Old Testament' in the Protestant Tradition," 122-23.
18. See Sanders, *From Sacred Story to Sacred Text*, 165, who points out that the canonical process depended on the community rather than church councils.
19. Sanders, *Canon and Community*, 12; see also Barr, *Holy Scripture*, 53-63.

In conclusion, I should like to make one practical suggestion. The three-year cycle of Scripture readings for the Eucharistic celebration was prepared by Roman Catholics and adopted by Lutherans and Presbyterians. It is, however, regrettable that in this lectionary the reading of the Prime Testament is not seen in its own right but as a background (often with imaginary associations) to the gospel. Thus the Christian in the worshipping community of the historic churches is encouraged to approach the Prime Testament reading solely from a Christian point of view. Perhaps in the future, liturgists and biblical scholars will be able to devise a Eucharistic liturgy in which our Jewish heritage is recognized in its own right. This could be achieved either by taking the second reading—a continuous reading usually taken from the Epistles—from the text of the Hebrew Bible, or by reading sections of the Bible in chronological order so that the congregation gains some appreciation of the development of salvation history. However, the best counsel would be to invite Jewish participants as consultants when the lectionary is revised.

Hebrew Bible *and* Old Testament: Textual Criticism in Service of Biblical Studies

JAMES A. SANDERS

The title of this book, *Hebrew Bible or Old Testament?* presents us starkly with the basic problem of what we study. The thinking world at large seems to be settling on the expression "Hebrew Bible" (*Biblia Hebraica*). One sees it now in Christian seminary catalogs. Yet Jews among themselves simply say "Bible" or use the acronym, *Tanakh*. Christians have become uncomfortable with "Old Testament," largely because we think Jews are uncomfortable with it, but also because some Christian scholars are reaching for a hermeneutic other than the traditional ones of Christocentrism or promise-fulfillment. A few Christian scholars and even a few Jewish scholars have recently focused exclusively on a theology of the Hebrew Bible.[1] And yet Jacob Neusner has persuaded not a few other scholars

---

1. See Knierim, "Task of Old Testament Theology"; the responses by others; and Knierim's response to them. See also Rendtorff, "'Biblical Theology,'" 40-43; and Tsevat, "Theology of the Old Testament," 33-59. See as well Levenson, "Why Jews Are Not Interested," 281-307.

that the real canon of Judaism is in the rabbinic corpus of
Formative Judaism and not in the Bible.[2]

The board of editors of the *Biblical Theology Bulletin*
decided a few years ago to experiment with the expressions
"First Testament" and "Second Testament," noting that the
solution is not without its own problems, but that it might offer
a viable alternative.[3] After all, while Hebrew Bible may vaguely
suffice as reference to the First or Old Testament of Protestants
and to the Bible of Jews, it is inadequate for Catholics and
Orthodox Christians. And those whose work includes focus on
the Septuagint cannot use the expression "Hebrew Bible"
everywhere they used to say "Old Testament." And we all feel a
little discomfort when we ignore the Aramaic portions of
the . . . thing!

Emanuel Tov recently remarked that we work in a field that
has no data base. He, Johann Cook, and the Ancient Biblical
Manuscript Center have begun to rectify the situation by
constructing computerized data bases of the Judaean scrolls.[4]
And that is in large measure the reason for the establishment of
the Ancient Biblical Manuscript Center, to provide at least a
raw but highly accessible data base on which we can all work
and no longer be dependent, as Barbara Aland of the Hermann
Kunst Stiftung recently wrote, on "chance knowledge" of
manuscripts.[5] This is a point to which we shall return, but one
might well ask, How does the question of what to call the very
elastic book we study relate to issues of textual criticism?

A beginning to an answer lies in the observation that even
if we should someday attain something like a complete raw

2. See Neusner, *Formative Judaism*. Orthodox Jews probably take the
Responsa as functionally canonical and Reform Jews only the Bible.

3. *Biblical Theology Bulletin* 17/2 (1987): 46-49.

4. Tov and Cook, "A Computerized Data Base ," 133-37; and Tov, "Hebrew
Biblical Manuscripts," 5-37.

5. Aland, "New Instrument and Method," 33-50.

data base in our field, with films of all extant biblical manuscripts available at Münster (in the case of the Second Testament) or at Claremont (in the case of both testaments), we shall still have only apographs with which to work. There is no such thing as a monograph, or an Urtext, of any biblical literature, a point underscored by the sensationalism attached to the Greek papyri found in Qumran Cave 7.[6] This observation obtains whether the reference is to texts or versions.

I suggest this as a starting point for what to call pre-Christian Scripture in part because that was where Martin Luther found himself when in 1523 he began his program of translation of the Old Testament. It is very interesting to start with Luther because the sixteenth and seventeenth centuries marked the beginnings of biblical criticism in which there was still some dialogue, or at least open disputation between Protestants and Catholics and a few Jews—a situation that would not return until a century ago. Luther's principle of *sola scriptura* began almost immediately to become problematic for him.[7] Without the magisterium and traditions of the church to fall back on, following Jerome's principle of *Hebraica Veritas* forced him to elaborate a hermeneutic of textual criticism and translation which, it would appear, he had not yet thought necessary. The hermeneutic, which he called *res et argumentum*, would provide for him the key both to choice of words, in the case of variants, and to choice of meaning of crucial words.[8] Words, he insisted must be in service of meaning, not meaning in service of words. *Res* for Luther was the gospel of Jesus Christ. *Argumentum* included three themes:

6. See Fitzmyer, "New Testament at Qumran," 119-23.
7. Apparently first stated clearly in the preface to the 1522 publication on his translation of the New Testament. See the *Weimar Ausgabe*, DB 6, 2-11.
8. See Barthélemy, *Critique textuelle*, *4-9. An English translation of the first five volumes of Orbis biblicus et orientalis (50/1-5), including *Critique textuelle* (vol. 1), is in process but not yet available.

oeconomia, politia, and *ecclesia.* If a passage did not accord with *ecclesia* or the gospel, then one dealt with it in terms of the political or economic systems of antiquity. Luther had great respect for Hebrew grammar and the great Jewish grammarians through the work of Elias Levita, but if a word in the text was multivalent then the meaning which accorded with the *res* of the gospel was to be chosen. If the Jewish grammarians and commentators gave the word a meaning not in accord with the gospel, the Christian interpreter and translator was to reject it and work with the grammar, altering vowel points where necessary, to make it do so.

By 1541 Luther had come to view some texts as corrupt.[9] Luther thus came to a basic hermeneutic of suspicion with regard to the Hebrew text as received and transmitted in Judaism. His suspicion of the work of the Massoretes he also learned in part from Levita.[10] He finally advised that Christian students of the text should modify vowel points, accents, conjugations, constructions, and meanings—in fact, anything outside Hebrew grammar itself—and turn it from Jewish interpretations toward accord with the gospel. It became his view that Jews had for fifteen hundred years turned the Bible away from witness to "our Messiah and our faith."[11] While he allowed for textual corruptions due to the incompetence of scribes and to the deformity of letters, as some earlier Christians had said, his suspicions of the history of transmission of the text since the first century deepened.

A much more moderate hermeneutic of suspicion had been evident already in medieval Jewish exegesis. As early as the

---

9. See "Vom Schem Hamphoras" in *Weimar Ausgabe* 53, 646ff.; and Barthélemy, *Critique textuelle,* *5.

10. Simon, *Histoire,* 132.

11. Barthélemy, *Critique textuelle,* *5-7. See Greenspahn, "Biblical Scholars, Medieval and Modern," 245-58.

ninth century Ismail al-Ukbari (c. 840) suggested that there was a scribal error at Gen. 46:15.[12] While Ibn Ezra appeared scandalized at the suggestion of an earlier grammarian that there were more than one hundred places in Scripture where a word should be replaced by another, he himself cited six of the same hundred. By the time of Yefet ben Ely, and certainly by the time of Judah Hayyug and David Qimḥi, the principle of substitution of one word for another was accepted practice where the text seemed otherwise to be incomprehensible.[13] Sanctes Pagnini, toward the beginning of Luther's program of translation (1526-29), published a grammar and a thesaurus refining the method. These were the great grammarians whom Luther and other Christians respected, to the degree that they respected the Hebrew grammar they had analyzed. The next two centuries would see almost complete denigration among Christians of the work of the Massoretes, especially the vowel points and the accents (טעמים). But among serious students of the text, Hebrew grammar, based precisely upon the transmitted text, was held in high regard. As Richard Simon went to pains to point out, the rabbinic and Qaraite grammarians had learned their art from their Arab neighbors, indeed, the greatest ones wrote their grammars and discourses in Judaeo-Arabic.[14]

THE SEVENTEETH CENTURY

J. Buxtorf, Sr., in 1620, challenged Levita's thesis that the work of the Tiberian Massoretes, especially in regard to the vowel points, had little historical value and was not authoritative.[15] He blamed the 1539 translation of Levita for

---

12. Barthélemy, *Critique textuelle*, *2; Simon, *Histoire*, 166.
13. Barthélemy, *Critique textuelle*, *2-3; Simon, *Histoire*, 167-69.
14. Simon, *Histoire*, 166ff. Aspiring students of First Testament textual criticism would be well advised to learn Judeo-Arabic in depth.
15. Simon, *Histoire*, 6, 136ff.

Luther's attitude toward the vowel points. Buxtorf defended the Massoretes, claiming that while the vowel points did not have divine or prophetic authority, they were received by tradition from high antiquity and should be respected lest Scripture become as malleable as wax.[16]

Louis Cappel, in his *Critica Sacra* of 1634, responded that the points had been invented five hundred years after Christ, and that the danger in ignoring them would be limited by literary context. J. Buxtorf, Jr., then took up where his father had left off and in his *Anticritica Sacra* of 1653 further defended the Massoretes as traditionalists of the first order.

Jean Morin, in a letter of 1653, in turn defended Cappel, not for being the Protestant heretic that he clearly was, but because his work showed precisely the importance of the church's magisterium and the falsehood of Luther's principle of *sola scriptura*.[17] Morin's hermeneutic, stated in his *Exercitationum*, would put Hebrew manuscripts at the service of the church's translations in order to clarify text and meaning but not to dominate or obfuscate their clear meaning. Hence, traditional versions should not be corrected on the basis of the Massoretic text since the Massoretic text may have become corrupt (after all, the Septuagint is much older), and the defects of the texts on which the traditional versions were made have since been authenticated by church usage. *Errore hominum providentia divina*, indeed!

Cappel, on the Protestant side, was consistent in stressing the importance of literary context. Not only would this not leave the unpointed consonantal text mere wax; contextual reading, on the contrary, should be the final arbiter of meaning of obscure words and passages. Whatever rendered "the most appropriate and useful sense" would always be the preferred

16. Barthélemy, *Critique textuelle*, *10ff; Simon, *Histoire*, 9.
17. Barthélemy, *Critique textuelle*, *17-20.

variant to choose. Warnings even from fellow Protestants that criticism had always followed the principle of *lectio difficilior* went unheeded. Cappel's principle of facilitating readings, it may be said, has been a mainstay of textual criticism until recently. While one may not finally agree with the younger Buxtorf, he needs to be heard, even today, in his challenge to Cappel:

> One would eventually come to the point that when a certain passage will not appear clear enough to a translator, to a professor, or to some critic, the latter will start to look about him to see if he could not find something whatever more appropriate, whether in the versions or in his own mind and capacity to invent conjectures. And thus will one become further removed from the traditional Hebrew reading for no matter what motive, or even without the least motive.[18]

Cappel followed very carefully wrought arguments in the second part of Buxtorf, Jr.'s *Anticritica,* as seen in his posthumously published *Notae Criticae,* and he was sometimes convinced by them. The remarkable thing is that much textual criticism, at least until quite recently, has not followed them. One need not agree with some of Buxtorf's basic suppositions and principles, as Simon indeed did not;[19] but one must agree that his warning to Cappel rings true as a prediction of what was to follow in much text-critical work for three centuries to come.

It might be noted that while Catholics on the whole felt secure in their second ground of truth, the church and its magisterium over against the Protestants' focus on Scripture, it is difficult to draw clear lines in all these debates between individual Protestant and Catholic scholars. What George Lindbeck has recently called the classic hermeneutics—what

18. Buxtorf, Jr., *Anticritica* (1653), 258; Barthélemy, *Critique textuelle,* *22.
19. Simon, *Histoire,* 9 and passim.

prevailed in the premodern period before the advent of
rationalism and empiricist literalism—bound all Christians
together. Scripture was constitutive of Christian communities
by a kind of *sensus fidelium*. They read Scripture "as a Christ-
centered narrationally and typologically unified whole in
conformity to a trinitarian rule of faith."[20] But, according to
Lindbeck, the Reformed churches after Calvin so focused on
finding "a single, all-embracing, and unchanging system of
doctrine in the Bible," that they became ritually impoverished
over against not only Catholics but also Lutherans. Their
disciplined reading and study of Scripture, and skill in its uses,
probably made them the most influential single group in
shaping what Lindbeck calls modernity.[21]

What emerges then out of the seventeenth-century debates
is a more or less clear distinction between Lutherans and
Calvinists, or those of the Reformed faith. The Reformed
churches of Zurich, Basel, Bern, and Geneva published in 1675
the *Formula Consensus Ecclesiarum Helveticarum
Reformatarum*, directed specifically, apparently, at Cappel's
school at Saumur. In it the vowel points were said to be
included also in the inspiration of Holy Scripture. What God
gave Moses and the prophets to write, God guarded over with
paternal affection, consonants and vowels, to the very hour of
the creation of the *Formula Consensus*. While they had
eventually to back down from such a rigid stance, it should be
noted that Lutherans, following Luther's own differentiated
views of the various portions of Scripture, never approached
such rigidity in defense of Luther's own principle of *sola
scriptura*.

By the middle of the seventeenth century, critics and
anticritics alike had agreed that if the autographs of Moses and

---

20. Lindbeck, "Scripture, Consensus, and Community," 5-24; see especially 7.
21. Lindbeck, "Scripture, Consensus, and Community," 10.

the prophets were available, they would be the norm, or true canon, for the text of the Hebrew Bible, indeed, of the Old Testament as well. The anticritics held that by a special divine assistance the Massoretic text had been preserved identical, or nearly so, to the autographs. The critics maintained that the available apographs contained serious errors and corruptions in a number of readings; some also held that there was evidence of different *Vorlagen* behind the Massoretic text and Septuagint traditions.

Benedict de Spinoza

A major contribution of the seventeenth century had been that of Benedict de Spinoza's *Tractatus Theologico-Politicus* (1670).[22] His was a free spirit indeed, condemned both by synagogue and church. In the background of his thinking were Thomas Hobbes and Isaac de La Peyrère. While Hobbes focused on what of the Pentateuch Moses actually contributed, de La Peyrère, a Calvinist who converted to Catholicism and knew Simon at the Oratoire, dismissed any hope of finding biblical autographs and stressed that critics must be content with copies of copies of literature that represented but abstracts and abbreviations of originals in the first place. De La Peyrère clearly wanted to diminish the authority of Scripture in order to put the Messiah and the salvation of the Church in bold relief. In this he followed Jean Morin's hermeneutic, and searched for prooftexts to support his messianic and christological views.

Spinoza reacted not only to de La Peyrère but to all theologians who, according to Spinoza, for the most part extorted from Scripture what passed through their heads. He insisted that true critics must liberate themselves from theological prejudices and develop a valid method for

22. Spinoza, *Tractatus*. Barthélemy, *Critique textuelle*, *40-46.

expositing Scripture, and that required elaborating an exact history of the formation of the text so that the thoughts of the original authors within their ancient contexts could be discerned. Spinoza was not the first to focus on original authorial intentionality, but he did so in such a way that his influence has been felt ever since. Out of those individuals' ideas could be extrapolated those doctrines and teachings on which they all agreed. Authority, for Spinoza, clearly rested in the intentions of the authors, much of which was lost in obscurity. Only what is intelligible remains authoritative, but this must be deemed sufficient for the salvation, or repose, of the soul. The rest is not worth the bother. Until such a history could be written, and he seriously doubted if one would ever be complete, Spinoza deemed the double commandment of love of God and love of neighbor to be the true Torah of God, and to be the common religion of all humankind. That was what was incorruptible, not some books called holy.

Richard Simon

Richard Simon took Spinoza seriously and wrote the *Histoire Critique du Vieux Testament*, published in Paris in 1678.[23] Though Simon mentions Spinoza's name only a few times in the "Préface de l'Auteur," it is clear from the first ten or so chapters that Simon was addressing issues that Spinoza had raised. Simon had access to all the efforts that had gone before and to the rich resources of the Oratoire and of the royal library. His was the mind needed at the end of the seventeenth century to make sense of all that had gone before in the abrupt starts and stops of attempts to establish biblical criticism as a fine art and a science. Spinoza's call for a critical history of the formation of the text was heeded by the man who could do the

---

23. See above, note 10.

most about it at the time. I disagree with Henri Margival that Simon was the father of biblical criticism.[24] He could have been, but he was not, simply because some of his major points were lost in the battles he had to fight with Bishop Bossuet and against the rationalist optimism of the eighteenth century. We cannot today agree with all his principles, but we can regret that some of the major ones have been largely overlooked in the three centuries since he wrote. Johann David Michaelis might rather be seen as the father of the kind of biblical criticism which has been practiced until quite recently.[25]

Simon responded to Spinoza's pessimism about recovering the history of the formation of the Bible with a two-fold hermeneutic. First, authority lies not in the intention of the individual authors which one might then appropriate through a harmonizing reductionism, but in the inspiration of Scripture by God's Holy Spirit continuing from the very beginnings of the creations of Scripture in all its parts, through to the closure and fixation of text. Second, while the Holy Spirit used the imagination and the intention of the prophets in their original settings, there were second and further meanings available for later times. These two points in his hermeneutic require considerable unpacking.[26]

Simon expressly did not agree with the Calvinists and anticritics that the Holy Spirit guarded with parental providence what the autographs had contained. His point was totally other. Simon spoke of the inspiration of "public scribes" who contributed to the texts in the process of their transmission; theirs was a prophetic authority equal to the

24. Margival, *Essai sur Richard Simon*, viii, passim. See Auvray, *Richard Simon*.

25. I am very much tempted to nominate Simon as the godfather of canonical criticism (as I understand it).

26. Simon, *Histoire*, "Préface de l'auteur," and passim.

original authors' authority.[27] The Spirit can valorize the
ignorance of original authors beyond their limited intentions.
(If some of this sounds like postmodern literary criticism, it is,
nonetheless, from Simon and from the late seventeenth
century.)[28] Two senses of a passage may be discerned, the
literal/historical and the spiritual, a further meaning. Some of
this is recognizable in the concept of the *sensus plenior* of
Scripture. A psalm was intended for an original *Sitz im Leben*,
but it was valid for totally different situations in later times. In
canonical criticism this is called the resignification of a passage;
and while Simon often wrote of the possibility of two senses of
a passage, there were other, further meanings beyond authorial
intentionality that were made valid in believing communities.

Simon stressed that it is impossible fully to understand
Christianity without a knowledge of Judaism and its history. In
addressing the issue of the value of consulting Jewish
understandings of Scripture, Simon boldly stated that the
authority God had given the Hebrew Republic through Moses
and the eighteen judges had never been withdrawn. In one
stroke Simon dealt with the problem of supersessionism, and
of the need of comparative Midrash. Comparative Midrash is
the exercise whereby one may discern the latitude early
believing communities allowed themselves in understanding
or resignifying a figure or passage of Scripture and the
hermeneutics whereby they did so. When then one reaches the
Second Testament and how Scripture, Septuagint or Hebrew,
functioned there, one has already a perspective on the function

27. Adumbrating the important statement about biblical scribal activity as a
part of the canonical text in Talmon, "Textual Study of the Bible," 321-400; as
well as the view of canonical criticism held by the present writer (see Sanders,
Canon and Community; and Sanders, *From Sacred Story to Sacred Text*, 153-
91). See also Talmon, "Heiliges Schrifttum und kanonische Bücher," 45-79.

28. See, e.g., Fowler, "Post-Modern Biblical Criticism," 8. And see above, note
20.

of that passage in Jewish believing communities up to that point. One can then truly discern so-called similarities and dissimilarities because one has built a data base of function of that passage up to its appearance in the New Testament. Simon's emphases on the continuing work of the Holy Spirit all along that path, and on the continuing authority within the Hebrew Republic, provide the base for the hermeneutic of canonical criticism when it focuses on canon as *norma normans* and not only as *norma normata*.

We must know, he wrote, both the literal and the developed meanings within Judaism and then within Christianity. When faced with the question of whether the Sanhedrin had divine authority to condemn Jesus, his response was that God can indeed use what we call corruption. Once more, *errore hominum providentia divina*, but this time much more fully thought through than by Morin. In the monotheizing hermeneutic of canonical criticism (as I understand it), Simon's point would be understood as perceiving that God is the God of life and death, risings and fallings, victories and defeats, protagonists and antagonists.[29]

While I would disagree that it is "inutile de rechercher . . . qui ont été les auteurs," canonical criticism (as I understand it) would applaud this significant challenge to Spinoza's idea of resting authority solely in the intentionality of the original individual authors. Simon's understanding of the further authority of the public scribes, who also contributed to the text and adapted it in some measure to their later situations, is also our understanding of the need to see canon and community in the same light and as inseparable.[30] The variants functioned in

---

29. See the writer's articles on "Canon (Old Testament)" forthcoming in the *Anchor Bible Dictionary*, and on "Deuteronomy" in Anderson, *Books of the Bible*, vol. 1, 89-102.

30. See above, note 27.

some believing communities though not in others, and it is important to know as many as there were, if possible, and to understand them in their textual contexts—another point that canonical criticism stresses, the need to appreciate the integrity of each manuscript or family of manuscripts before pillaging it or them to correct what appears to be a corruption or error in another. Thus Simon's respect of the Septuagint witness brought him to criticize even Jerome: "Je n'excuse pas même Saint Jérôme, qui n'a pas rendu aux Septante toute la justice qu'il leur devoit."[31]

Finally, Simon disagreed with Spinoza's distinction between reason and enthusiasm. Spinoza viewed prophetic authority, that is genuine authority, as practically devoid of reason. Whereas Spinoza minimized the contribution of individual reason and imagination, Simon stressed how the Holy Spirit used such gifts first in the so-called original contributors and then all along the path of the formation of the Bible, and, to be sure, all along the Church's understanding of Scripture in the magisterium since canonization. This was the reason he agreed with Spinoza that a critical history of the formation of the biblical texts had to be attempted. While canonical criticism must disagree with Simon's understanding of the goal of the Spirit being only the New Testament's messianic, second meaning, making the New Testament in effect the key to understanding what the Spirit was doing, Simon alone provided an adequate response to Spinoza in his stress on the continuing work of the Spirit all along the path of formation of the texts, not guarding original readings in their purity, but inspiring the "public scribes" who added to texts as well as subtracting from them, adapting them in various though limited ways for their later communities. Of course,

31. Simon, *Histoire*, 232.

there is a sense in which Luther and Simon were right that Christians would read the First Testament in terms of its goal being the gospel, if that means that we grant that rabbinic Jews would read it in terms of its goal being rabbinic Judaism.[32] In that case we would need to say "Hebrew Bible *and* Old Testament."

THE EIGHTEENTH CENTURY

The eighteenth century began with the rationalist optimism in these matters for which it is noted otherwise. Hard work combined with intelligence and reason would open a clear path to the establishment of the best text possible. Numerous German scholars worked on as many manuscripts as were available to them. Johann H. Michaelis studied manuscripts in and around Erfurt and published his results in a *Biblia Hebraica* with critical apparatus published in Halle in 1720; Theodor Christoph Lilienthal worked on those in Königsberg which he published in 1770; Georg Johann Ludwig Vogel worked on those available in Helmstadt which he published in 1765; and then entered the probable father of textual criticism as we have known it since, Johann David Michaelis who published his work on the manuscripts available in Kassel beginning in 1771.[33]

Simon had noted that while nearly anyone could amass variants from the various printed editions of the Hebrew Bible, very few people had the resources available to consult "les vieux manuscrits."[34] Cappel had worked almost exclusively, apparently, on printed editions for his *Critica Sacra*; and Morin, who had access to the rich library of the Oratoire in Paris

32. See Barr, *Old and New in Interpretation*, 26-33; Sanders, *From Sacred Story to Sacred Text*, 9-39, and 125-91.
33. Barthélemy, *Critique textuelle*, *28.
34. Simon, *Histoire*, 117.

consulted very few manuscripts and did so only with negligence. It was Charles François Houbigant who exploited in depth the holdings of the Oratoire, as well as other scattered manuscripts, to publish his magnificent *Biblia Hebraica* in four in-folio volumes in 1753.[35] Houbigant, of course, had the polyglots of London (Walton) and of Paris, which provided him comparisons with the Samaritan Pentateuch and its targum, as well the Peshitto.

But Houbigant largely disregarded vowel points, the accents, and the *massora*, arguing that human faculties of memory were incapable of retaining all the minutiae. The Buxtorfs had agreed, ironically, on this point, arguing that they must therefore have come from sacred authors, at least from Ezra. Houbigant took the other position that they derived only from the Massoretes who invented all but the consonants.

This was the stage onto which the young Oxford scholar, Benjamin Kennicott, entered to begin his work of collation. His first publications (of 1753 and 1759) were limited to the manuscripts available in Oxford, Cambridge, and the British Museum. He then sought royal patronage and traveled broadly in Europe engaging collaborators, and he finally published in 1776 and 1780 the two volumes which continue to be consulted in textual criticism today.[36] Kennicott's work came under severe criticism, especially from Johann David Michaelis.[37] Not only had Kennicott disregarded the vowel points and accents, he also showed preference for facilitating readings. He had been persuaded, apparently, not only by the arguments of Cappel and Houbigant. He also agreed with Morin.

35. Barthélemy, *Critique textuelle*, *24-28.

36. Benjamin Kennicott, *Vetus Testamentum Hebraicum*. See Goshen-Gottstein, "Hebrew Biblical Manuscripts," 243-90.

37. In the *Göttingische Anzeigen von gelehrten Sachen* (1760) and in his *Orientalische und Exegetische Bibliothek* (1771); Barthélemy, *Critique textuelle*, *30-32.

J. B. de Rossi published in 1784-98 four volumes on some 1,793 codices which Kennicott and his team had missed.[38] Still little work would be done on oriental manuscripts until the work of Paul Kahle on Leningradensis, the Cairo Codex of the Prophets, and Orientalis 4445. Kahle, by the way, apparently agreed with Levita and Cappel on the late date of the vowel points. Then came the discovery of the Qumran manuscripts, which seemed to confirm the opinion of Morin and Cappel that the *Vorlage* of the Septuagint represented a different textual tradition from that of the Massoretic text.

APOGRAPHS AND THE TEXT

We indeed have but apographs with which to work. This is but a part of what Reinhold Niebuhr called the ambiguity of human reality. For one suspects that if an autograph were to be found two things would happen. First, its authenticity would be immediately disputed. And second, by some criteria, some critics would find it inferior to what we already have. This will not deter us in efforts to try to identify autographs, as in the case of Qumran Cave 7. But what we actually have are apographs of texts and versions, each having its own story, each having a history of textual and literary transmission lying back of it and its many *Vorlagen*.

But there is a new situation today in which to view those apographs. For now we have copies of copies in a new sense, that is, there is now the possibility of having image-enhanced photographs gathered and collected in one place so that comparative study can be carried out in ways never done before. In addition, computer technology permits more and more accurate collating of the manuscripts to form a significant data base on which to make more sound judgments. When we

38. Rossi, *Variae lectiones Veteris Testamenti.*

began our work in Freudenstadt on the some five thousand textual problems given us by the United Bible Societies, we developed an understanding of what we were doing in terms of the calls enunciated by Johann David Michaelis, Paul Volz, Henrik Samuel Nyberg, and Rudolf Kittel for an international and interconfessional team to work out concepts and methods for textual criticism.[39] The United Bible Societies had brought us together for one reason: however, we set about our work not only to do the task asked of us, but also to attempt precisely to answer the call Michaelis had made some three hundred years earlier. It is clear from the various reviews of our work that it has not created a consensus.[40] And I will not make this the occasion to mount a defense of what we have done. On the contrary, we continue to learn.

One of the lessons we can learn from the history of textual criticism since Luther is the respect that scholars aware of their work have had for the rabbinic and Qaraite grammarians; and the work of our colleague Dominique Barthélemy in that regard may well be the strongest contribution we shall have made. I think it safe to say that no prior effort has probed so deeply into the great grammarians on so many problems.[41] It requires an in-depth working knowledge of Hebrew and

39. Barthélemy, *Critique textuelle*, *60-70. See Greenberg's perceptive review of Barthélemy, *Critique textuelle* in *Jewish Quarterly Review* 78 (1987): 137-40: "Since biblical literature was produced by, and transmitted in faith communities, it is not permissible to ignore that fact in reconstituting its text. . . . This work . . . will serve its highest purpose if it compels the critic, who alone can appreciate it and judge it, to confront the elementary questions of his profession" (p. 140).

40. See, e.g., Albrektson's critique, *"Difficilior lectio probabilior,"* 5-18; Ulrich's notice in *Bulletin of the International Organization for Septuagint and Cognate Studies* 16 (1983): 5; and his "Canonical Process." The last would provide a good base on which to have a genuine dialogue about where textual criticism should go now, and especially about its relation to higher criticism.

41. So Greenberg's review of Barthélemy, 138: "Jewish scholarship has not canvassed Jewish exegesis for text critical purposes on this scale."

Aramaic in all their phases and of Judaeo-Arabic. Very valuable also was the work of Norbert Lohfink and his assistant on the committee, Clemens Locher, in terms of more recent critical work on the passages dealt with, as well as all the accumulated knowledge from archaeology, architecture, geography, ancient near-eastern military history, flora and fauna, metalurgy, etc. No stone was consciously left unturned in any of these areas. And we had the cooperation of the scholars working on the Judaean Desert scrolls and fragments, especially Frank Cross, Patrick Skehan, and Eugene Ulrich.

A direct result of our labors was the decision in 1977, before we had completed our basic work in Freudenstadt, to leave New York to go to Claremont to help found the Ancient Biblical Manuscript Center. It was clear that there had to be a place where image-enhanced films, and eventually computerized and digitized data bases of all the manuscripts, texts, and versions, could be well preserved and available and accessible for full comparative study. The technology is there, both in photography and climate control, for indefinite preservation of film. The observations made earlier about how collations and apparatus have been compiled still obtained; the scholar worked on the manuscripts available. Even Kennicott and de Rossi collated only European manuscripts, and Kahle's work early in this century on the Oriental was only a beginning. The discovery of the Judaean manuscripts made it mandatory to broaden the data base as far as possible, and modern technology was developing the means for doing so. Barbara Aland of Münster has stated the case very well:

> In the history of our field of scholarship, by now a very long history, all work done in textual criticism of the New Testament has encountered a problem that still remains unsolved today. Each editor . . . could choose for the basis of his edition only those manuscripts which he knew by chance. Starting with the first editors, Erasmus and Ximenes, and continuing up to the great ones of our discipline, Tischendorf, Westcott and Hort, and von Soden, it

was the general practice to use what was individually known. . . .
Up to our times the following unquestionably holds true: the
selection of manuscripts on which we base our work—especially in
the field of the miniscules—is founded on our chance knowledge of
these codices.[42]

While textual criticism of the First Testament is configured
differently from that of the Second, the same observations hold
true. At the Manuscript Center we intend to correct that
situation. We have the intention, and the acquisition program
in place, whereby eventually, as funds are available, to make
accessible all the manuscripts, texts, and versions pertinent to
the task of textual criticism (except those restricted by the
source, such as unpublished Dead Sea Scroll films). The
Biblisches Institut in Münster has collected some fifty-three
hundred Greek New Testament manuscripts; that category
grows as each new papyrus is discovered.[43] The Manuscript
Center by the close of the millennium hopes to have twenty
thousand manuscripts, mainly texts, of both testaments, as
money becomes available. It will take perhaps another twenty
years thereafter to come anywhere close to having substantially
what is extant, but there are already core collections in both
testaments. And whenever a scholar proposes a project of
research on nonbiblical but cognate manuscripts, we interrupt
the basic acquisition program to collect what is specifically
needed. The present situation of scholars being dependent on
prior collations and apparatuses, or even on critical editions
that have been shaped and formed by variable biases,
competences, and interests of earlier editors can be corrected.
The day of perpetuating earlier errors and biases can be brought
to a close.

42. See above, note 5.
43. Aland and Aland, *Text of the New Testament*, 72ff.

The lesson learned from the work of our United Bible Societies Committee that impressed me the most is the need to respect the integrity of each manuscript, or at least family of manuscripts, before pillaging it to correct a different one. The relative textual fluidity characteristic of the manuscripts, texts, and versions (and presumably their *Vorlagen*) that date before stabilization of text and canon requires keeping in mind the communities from which they came and the needs they served.[44] This is the case in New Testament textual criticism as well, where relative fluidity is also a characteristic of the textual situation before the fourth century.[45] Thinking in terms of scribal errors and corruptions should be a final resort and should come only after careful work on the literary and historical context of the text in which the variants occur.

Respect should precede suspicion. Where possible, the fuller contexts of each variant textual reading, including the community from which it came, if that is at all possible, should be studied to see whether a seeming variant was a true one or a reading engendered for other reasons, such as the hermeneutics of the tradent or translator, his or her conceptuality of what was going on in the larger context of the text, and his or her desire to serve the need for understanding by the community for which the copy or translation was being made.[46]

44. Note the common emphases in Simon, Talmon, and the writer; see above, note 27.

45. See Aland in "A New Instrument and Method," 42: "The early manuscripts also have a higher degree of independence than the texts copied very strictly in Byzantium later on." The same point was made in Sanders, "Text and Canon," 373-94.

46. This should be as much a concern in the ongoing work of establishing the history of the text as that of discerning original intentions. Simon's *Histoire* truly initiated this continuing task. Objections that there are dark periods must be steadily addressed by further work, such as the project now proposed by Talmon to write a history of Judaism in the Persian period.

Three factors need to be identified, where possible: hermeneutics, conceptuality, and community needs. Ancient copyists and translators, like their modern counterparts, wanted their work appreciated. They wanted their communities to understand the text; that was why they took on such labor. Of course, it was *their* understanding of the text they tried to convey. Modern critics and translators have the same aspirations. In the case of modern scholarship, a sociology of knowledge may be necessary for us to be able to discern whether the community for which we ultimately labor is the scholarly guild or the faith community. The self-identity of the scholar is a factor in the work we do; the current debates in this regard are not merely academic exercises.[47]

In order to appreciate communities' understanding of the text, full literary contexts of texts or translations must be studied to see the role that the apparent variant played in the whole passage and to understand how it served the larger conceptuality lying back of the text, as well as the hermeneutic at play in the recreation of the text in the receptor language, or in the new copy being made. Discernment of the conceptuality of the larger literary context can be arrived at by the steadily improving methods of structural analysis being developed by my colleague, Rolf Knierim, and by his colleagues in the *Forms of Old Testament Literature* (*FOTL*) project.[48] What was learned on the text-critical project of the United Bible Societies has been matched by what has been learned since the move to Claremont. My students are required to do careful macro- and microstructural analyses of their work in comparative Midrash. A student who recently defended his dissertation on a detailed comparison of the three forms in which the Book of Esther is

47. As cited in note 28 above.
48. R. Knierim and G. Tucker, eds. (Grand Rapids, Mich.: Eerdmans), 24 volumes projected, 5 published so far (end of 1988).

available in Greek (O', L, Jos) did detailed literary analyses of O' and L and was thereby able to account for almost every plus, minus, and so-called variant among them. These were then compared with the Massoretic text of Esther with the question left open as to whether it represented a form of Esther earlier than those in Greek, or not.[49] Another student did a tradition analysis of the components of the Gibeon story of Solomon's dream (1 Kings 3:2-15) and then a study of its *Nachleben* through Chronicles, the Old and later Greek versions, the Targumim, the Peshitta, and the Vulgate, then its pilgrimage into Qohelet, Wisdom of Solomon, and Q (Luke). He did a careful structural analysis of each, noting the hermeneutics involved in each resignification.[50] Stanley Walters has recently defended the integrity of the two stories of Hannah, the one in the Septuagint and the other in the Massoretic text.[51] Once one has discerned the integrity of each, it becomes very difficult to pillage one to "correct" the other. The recent publication of the correspondence and debate among four textual scholars of the two accounts of the encounter between David and Goliath is an example of the kind of respect needed in such cases before pillaging begins.[52] Johann Lust concluded for the four that "both versions are valuable ones and stand in their own right. The one should not be corrected by the other."[53] A number of modern versions now translate the Hebrew Esther in the canonical section and a full Greek Esther in the Apocrypha.

Whether the case must rest there or not depends on further consideration and on other factors. Theoretically, one must

---

49. Dorothy, "The Books of Esther." Another dissertation, by J. McCrory, indicates a possible break in the impasse of the history of formation of both the Massoretic text and the Septuagint version of Exodus chapters 35-40.

50. Carr, "Royal Ideology."

51. Walters, "Hannah and Anna," 385-412.

52. Barthélemy, Gooding, Lust, and Tov, *Story of David and Goliath.*

53. Barthélemy, Gooding, Lust, and Tov, *Story of David and Goliath,* 156.

allow for a later, completely unknown author/editor to have
had the true literary genius which a given structural analysis
exposes. Then one must go on to a macrostructure of the fuller
contexts of each of the variant accounts to see if that same
genius was at work elsewhere. Often we shall have to confess
that we do not know whether the literary genius we can
perceive in our present context is the one that our students, or
theirs, will perceive. William F. Albright is quoted as saying
that the archaeologist should leave more of a *tel* undug than
dug, because the next generations will have sharper tools to use
and better questions to ask of the *tel* with all its ancient secrets.
My colleague, Eugene Ulrich, has pondered some of these
issues in a recent study on "Double Literary Editions of Biblical
Narratives."[54] And he poses good questions. I am not sure
whether simply translating for a community of faith will decide
the issue. In that case, conceivably, the Greek Esther only
should be translated for Christian Bibles and the Hebrew Esther
only for Jewish Bibles; but that would be an impoverishment
for both at this late stage. The western churches, Catholic and
Protestant, all inherit Jerome's principle of *Hebraica Veritas* and
must work with it in the best and improving text-critical mode
possible. One might ask whether, as we move into the twenty-
first century, those churches are not ready for a pluriformity of
texts where double editions are available, even in translations.
We have the Massoretic text pluriformity of two sets of Ten
Commandments, as well as Samuel-Kings and Chronicles in
the First Testament (besides numerous doublets in prose and
poetry), and four Gospels in the Second. The United Bible
Societies in Stuttgart has entertained a proposal to provide
modern critically based translations of the Septuagint.
Marguerite Harl and others have begun to do so in French.[55]

54. Ulrich, "Double Literary Editions."
55. Harl, *La Bible d'Alexandrie*.

The work of the United Bible Societies' committee is well-suited to establish a conservatively based "best critical text" for translations of the First Testament. We chose to work only on the Hebrew of Esther, Jeremiah, Proverbs, Exodus chapters 35-40, and Ezekiel chapters 40-48 precisely because of the quite different inner-literary developments in the Greek and Hebrew of those quite obvious cases. And where there were double literary editions we tended to respect each, and hence usually chose the Hebrew form with its own *Wortschatz*.[56] Thus our work has a conservative cast as Albrektson and Greenberg have noted—conservative in the sense not of Christian theological *Tendenz* (in that case we might have chosen many more Septuagint readings), but conservative in the Massoretic sense. One must concede that where such considerations did not come into play, we chose a fair number of non-Massoretic text readings.

CONCLUSIONS

I conclude these observations by noting that there is a new day in textual criticism marked by (a) the availability and accessibility, due to modern technology, of as much as there is extant of texts to work on; (b) revisions in the history of transmission of the Hebrew and Greek texts; (c) full respect for the integrity of differing manuscript traditions and the ancient believing communities from which they come; and (d) new techniques such as literary and structural analysis whereby to discern as much as is possible the reality and conceptuality lying

56. There are portions of the Septuagint which are targumic translations based on an apparently proto-Massoretic text, as in the case of Isaiah and some of the Minor Prophets; other portions are formal equivalence translations (e.g., the Pentateuch), even literalist or Theodotionic (e.g., Qohelet); the so-called double editions, of course, involve literary as well as textual histories, as well as a case like the Septuagint version of Proverbs.

back of the work of our tradent ancestors, both copyists and translators, and of their *Vorlagen*. The new day and the new skills do not preclude some basic questions that will still plague us, such as how close to some kind of autograph all these apographs and our carefully wrought and improving text-critical methods will permit us to approximate. We will and must have a continuing passion to hear original voices where possible, but we will need to ask what authority we attribute to each layer of textual formation and transmission.

One might envisage a round table in the center of which would be a biblical text, perhaps Isa. 28:16. Around the table one might imagine numerous readers: first there would be the First Isaiah as discerned by biblical historical criticism, then members of the school of Isaiah such as deutero-Isaiah and Habakkuk, there would be the Septuagint and Old Latin Isaiah, and the Vulgate Isaiah, the Syriac Isaiah, and the Targumim, all those who quote and allude to the passage in early Judaism including 11QIs and the apostle Paul, indeed any who quoted or alluded to Isa. 28:16 within the period of early canonical process. That should be quite a conversation! And it would afford a good perspective on the breadth of resignification that a canonical passage may support. Even so, I would want to give a weighted vote to the meanings of Isa. 28:16 itself as discerned by scholarship since the Enlightenment—as many as that might be; for so-called original meanings often change as scholarship evolves in its increased knowledge of the Iron Age and in the methods it uses in exegesis. But everyone should be heard, or at least not be ridiculed as succeeding generations of scholars come and go.

We must at the very least put respect for the work of our ancestors (even recent ones!) in the "traditioning-process" before suspicion. We may end up with more pluriformity than ecumenism can bear, or we may arrive at a state of humility and respect for one another and our various current traditions.

Whether we restrict our understanding to the Hebrew Bible and the best readings of that we can achieve, or if we think of the more elastic Prime or First Testament in its various forms and with its greater pluriformity, we need to adopt a posture of learning and listening to others' stories, texts, and traditions, familiar perhaps to each in other forms, which can mean enrichment for all. The theological ground of such a state might well be the recognition that the true Reality which lies behind of all our apographs is beyond the grasp or comprehension of any one line of tradition, but has spoken in many and sundry ways to our ancestors of old.[57]

We already have modern translations that put the Massoretic text of Esther in the Old Testament and a Greek Esther in the Apocrypha or deuterocanonical section. Why not also have the Massoretic text of Daniel in the Old Testament and a Greek Daniel in the Apocrypha?[58] We could go further and supply translations of the differing stories of Anna and Hannah, the latter in the text and the former in the margin (as is done in some translations for John 8:1-11 and the long ending of Mark); the same could be done with selected cases of literary doublets such as those in the so-called Lucianic Samuel, the night vision of Solomon in 1 Kings chapter 3, the death of Josiah perhaps, and even of significant portions of Septuagint Isaiah where it differs considerably as in Isaiah chapter 6. These could be judiciously and carefully chosen so that faithful Jews and Christians, as well as secular readers, could see the

57. See Sanders, "Challenge of Fundamentalism," 12-30.

58. Along with Jerome's principle of *Hebraica Veritas* we have also inherited his unfortunate solution of putting the larger pluses of the Greek Esther and Daniel in the Apocrypha as "additions," almost eliminating respect for the Septuagint, as Richard Simon lamented. See above, note 31.

pluriformity we truly inherit instead of only what some scholars think most approximates a supposed original. Again, such respect for the pluriformity we inherit would not eliminate but would include a continuing passion to strive for original readings.

What is needed is a new *phronesis* for the twenty-first century. I have called that *phronesis* "monotheizing pluralism" —God is One: that is, reality has ontological and ethical integrity, even while we humans are many, separated by differing identities and traditioning processes. That *phronesis* might be expressed by stressing reading our texts in a global context instead of denominational contexts. A beginning would indeed be made by reading any of our texts, even when alone, as though Jews and Christians were present. But that context should be expanded globally so that Muslims and Buddhists, men and women, and all races would become the context in which we seek understanding of our texts and traditions, and of ourselves in them.

Can we not at least pretend that God is One? If we do so enough, we might come truly and significantly to believe that God *is* One, with all that that could mean for living in the twenty-first century's global village. That would be a hermeneutic of respect indeed!

Jewish, Christian, and Empirical Perspectives on the Text of Our Scriptures

EUGENE ULRICH

When we Jews and Christians study the Hebrew Bible or the Old Testament, do we share a common reading? Do we bring to the text the same or different questions and presuppositions? The answers, as we are all aware, would not be the same in every era. I believe we are fortunate to be living in a generation that is ripe for such questions—a generation in which the issues can profitably be raised in a mutually respectful and hopeful setting, and with realistic promise that constructive advances can be made.

This paper focuses on the subject of the *text* of the Bible— together with the closely related issues of manuscripts, textual criticism, the work of the Massoretes, and canon. If we agree to the most hopeful aspirations expressed in this volume and then sit down to work together, What text would we read? What form of that text would we agree to examine, before we begin to interpret? Would it be a simple or problematic task to determine which form of the biblical text we read? I wish to explore some of the difficult questions at the scholarly and pastoral levels that must be addressed and answered—or ignored—prior to the reading and interpretation of the biblical text.

THE SIGNIFICANCE OF THE QUMRAN SCROLLS

At the outset, I would like to insert a brief comment on the significance of the Qumran scrolls, since these scrolls have opened the door to a roomful of ancient evidence of which we were unaware before the middle of this century. We have important new evidence concerning the text of the Bible that requires us to rearrange the stage upon which we and our communities study and use the Bible in academic and liturgical settings.

There are about two hundred fragmentary biblical manuscripts among the Qumran scrolls. They all predate the fall of the Jerusalem Temple in 70, and thus they antedate by a thousand years what had been our oldest Hebrew manuscripts of the Bible. They exert two very important controls on our knowledge of the history of the biblical text. First, they show that the medieval texts we had known, and from which our vernacular Bibles are translated, are in the main faithfully transmitted from antiquity. Second, they display a measured variety in texts and in textual families during the Second Temple period, which some scholars had already conjectured on the basis of the versions and quotations in rabbinic, New Testament, and early Church sources. For our purposes, we should note that the Massoretic text is *only one form* of the Bible as it had existed and had been accepted in the believing communities prior to the First Jewish Revolt against Rome (in 66-74) and perhaps up to the Second Revolt (in 132-135). In short, the Massoretic text is documented as *a faithful witness* to the ancient biblical text, but the fact is also documented that the

Massoretic text is *only one of the textual forms* of the ancient biblical text.

SOME HELPFUL DISTINCTIONS

When I was pursuing doctoral studies, I gradually came to realize that my views were much closer to those of the other students with whom I was studying (whatever their religious backgrounds) than they were to those of a number of people within my own Catholic tradition. In further conversations with some of my fellow students, I found that they, too, had experienced the same phenomenon. That ecumenical setting can serve as the springboard to several helpful distinctions.

One distinction contrasts empirical and dogmatic study. Empirical study pursues an inductive path and aims at leading to logical conclusions. It can truly be *fides quaerens intellectum* if that *fides* is understood as basic faith open to honest revision insofar as the data demand revision. Such empirical endeavors can be contrasted with dogmatic or confessional study which pursues a deductive path. Here the *fides quaerens intellectum* is understood less as basic faith open to revision than as traditional or customary forms or vehicles through which that basic faith has found expression. It is a difficult question how much Jews and Christians are, or should be, open to revision of ideas based on what we can learn from each other.

A second distinction can be made between convictions that are formed predominantly by reason (in this connection the term *critics*, used by James A. Sanders, seems apt) and convictions that are formed predominantly by faith (the term *anticritics* may be apt but may stir waters unnecessarily; would *noncritics* be better?). There is, of course, a wide and complex spectrum from "pure reason" to "blind faith." We all operate with presuppositions, we all operate from our personal and communal worldview. Some attempt more than others to move beyond a worldview circumscribed by the religious community within which we were born and to have our worldview intellectually accountable to the wider arena created by the results of "objective" academic or scientific study.

A third distinction involves the difference between individuated personalities as opposed to the difference between specifically confessional stances. This distinction thus asks whether differing views are due, on the one hand, to individual factors, such as academic training, personal outlook (whether conservative or liberal, traditional or innovative, etc.) or, on the other hand, to one's being Jewish or Christian as such. We are all a complex mixture of inherited qualities, indoctrination, life experiences, educational paths, career or vocational goals, and personally synthesized "life-wisdom." In a recent symposium organized by Shemaryahu Talmon, "The Hebrew Bible—From Literature to Canon,"[1] there were wide differences in views on canon; but my sense was that those differences were predominantly due to our individual scholarly orientations and experience rather than to our religious or doctrinal views.

A fourth distinction highlights the difference between the official canon and our functional canons. My suspicion is that for many Christians, the New Testament really functions as the important part of the Bible and as the way to interpret the Old Testament. For some Jews, too, the Mishnah and Talmud function as part of the canon and as the only proper way to interpret the Hebrew Bible.

These distinctions will be helpful in reviewing four areas of Sanders' paper, each of which highlights an issue that rages in discussions of text-critical methodology.

---

1. Held at the National Humanities Center in Research Triangle Park, North Carolina, April 27-29, 1988.

THE ORIGINAL TEXT

People often seek the original text, and the assumption is that such a text existed or exists, that we know what it means, and that we might have the possibility to attain it. In light of the four-phase history of the Hebrew text proposed by the Hebrew University Bible Project,[2] of course, *original text* might mean at least five different things: first, the original form of each unit of the text as it was first produced by its individual author (literary work prior to the HUBP's Phase 1); second, the original text of a complete book as it left the hand of the last major author or redactor (Phase 1); third, the original text as it was at that stage of development when a community accepted it as the authoritative text (some would say canonical text) and as it can be documented by extant manuscripts (Phase 2); fourth, the consonantal text of the rabbinic Bible (Phase 3); and fifth, the Massoretic text understood by rabbinic Judaism as the traditional text (Phase 4). There are many progressive steps between these phases to which one might apply the term *original text*.

Though the four phases are distinct conceptually, in practice, because of the nature of scribal creativity, the boundary lines are often far from clear.[3] At times the only difference between Phase 1 and Phase 2 is due to accidents of history (one text with a certain reading survives; another with a predictable variant does not).[4]

Of particular interest in the search for the elusive original text is Phase 4, the Massoretic text. Do some Jews and Christians tenaciously cling to the Massoretic text because they believe it

2. The phases are: "(1) that of the Urtext; (2) the accepted texts; (3) the received text; and (4) the Massoretic Text"; see Sanders, *From Sacred Story to Sacred Text*, 133.

3. See Ulrich, "Horizons," 613-36, especially 615-19.

4. Cf. Ulrich, "Canonical Process."

perfectly represents revelation given at Sinai (תורה מסיני)?
Because the Massoretic text is the *original* text? Because the
Massoretic text is the *best preserved* version? Because the
Massoretic text is the *final edition* of the set of biblical books?
None of these suggestions turns out to be accurate for the text as
a whole.

With reference to the Sinaitic revelation, let us distinguish
between the revelation itself and certain variants in its individual wording. The religious conviction that identifies the
Torah with the wording in the Massoretic text was formulated
in an era when it was presumed that the Hebrew text existed in
only one form, when there was no consciousness of a distinction between differing forms of the Hebrew text. Now that evidence from biblical manuscripts written in the era between
Moses and the Massoretes sheds more light on the wording of
the Torah, perhaps we should consider reformulating our conviction. It is possible that we have available an even more perfect formulation of the wording of the Torah which had been
copied so many times over the intervening millennia by very
careful, but not infallible, scribes.[5]

Text-critical information provides similar light on the other
three questions listed above. First, consider that the Massoretic
edition of Jeremiah is demonstrably secondary to the earlier
edition of that book in the Hebrew text of 4QJer[b] and the Greek
translation of it in the Septuagint.[6] A similar situation occurs
in 1 Samuel chapters 17–18: the David-Goliath episode as found
in the Septuagint is a faithful translation of a Hebrew edition of

5. Talmon ("The Old Testament Text," 159-99, especially 185) notes that
"According to rabbinic testimony, even the model codices that were kept in the
Temple precincts—the ᶜazarah—not only exhibited divergent readings, but
represented conflicting text-types." See also Talmon, "Three Scrolls of the
Law," 14-27.
   6. See Tov, "Some Aspects of the Textual and Literary History," 145-67.

the story that is earlier and shorter than the second, composite edition now found in the Massoretic text.[7] The earlier editions of Jeremiah and the David-Goliath episode found in the Septuagint, as well as the numerous secondary readings throughout the Massoretic text, demonstrate that the latter is not uniformly the original text. Second, the not infrequent errors or corruptions in the Massoretic text amply display that it is not uniformly the best preserved text. And third, the later editions of certain books, e.g., as exemplified in 4QpaleoExod[m] and 4QSam[a] (at 1 Samuel chapters 1–2) from Qumran,[8] demonstrate that the edition of those books preserved in the Massoretic text is not the final edition produced by the Jewish community in the Second Temple period.

All of this points to the fact that evidence prior to the stabilization of the wording of the Massoretic text (e.g., the Qumran scrolls and the ancient versions translated from Hebrew texts in antiquity) now demonstrates that the Massoretic text is a faithful witness to one, but only one, textual form of each of the biblical books as they reached the end of the Second Temple period.

Further examination of the Massoretic text of various books raises the serious question whether the rabbis' selection of the varied collection of texts we call the Massoretic text was conscious or accidental. More research is needed on this question, though the evidence suggests that at the level of religious authority the selection of the Massoretic text was conscious, but at the textual level it was accidental. That is, the rabbis used

7. Barthélemy, Gooding, Lust, and Tov, *Story of David and Goliath.* Both in theory and in examination of the data, the arguments by Lust and Tov—that the Septuagint is the earlier version—are persuasive (in contrast to those of Barthélemy and Gooding).

8. See Skehan, "Exodus," 182-87; and Sanderson, *Exodus Scroll from Qumran.* See also Cross, "New Qumran Biblical Fragment," 15-26.

Hebrew scrolls of each of the books (as opposed to Greek scrolls which Christians characteristically used) and decided that these were to be held as the sacred texts. But examination of the specific textual forms of the individual books (e.g., Samuel and Hosea) indicates that the religious-authority selection just described was not founded on a textual conviction that these texts were superior to other Hebrew forms of the text.[9] Moreover, the variant biblical citations in early rabbinic writings suggest that even if certain early rabbis did choose a specific textual form of the biblical books, that decision was not reflected in the usage of later rabbis. The same is true for early Christian authors: if the Church, or certain authorities within the Church, did choose a specific textual form of the biblical books, that decision was likewise not reflected in the biblical citations by subsequent Christian writers during the early centuries.

Thus, the Massoretic text is not simply to be equated with the original text in any simple sense. If we want to adopt the form of the text endorsed by rabbinic Judaism, then we should center on the Massoretic text; but we must know that the Massoretic text is not identical with the text of the early rabbis.

If we want to adopt the best preserved text, or the best text that we can attain with extant manuscripts and text-critical methods (with or without conjectural emendation), then we will strive for a critically established text. That text will agree often with the form in the Massoretic text, but it will also agree at times with other forms attested in the Septuagint, Syriac, Qumran, or other manuscripts. Occasionally, it will agree with

9. Even Childs, who opts strongly for the Massoretic text, agrees that "the subsequent status accorded the Massoretic text did not derive necessarily from its being the best, or the most original, Hebrew text. Its choice as the canonical text [sic] was determined often by broad sociological factors and internal religious conflicts (cf. Geiger), and not by scholarly textual judgments" (Introduction to the Old Testament, 103).

none of the extant texts, because most textual critics will acknowledge that at certain points all of our manuscript witnesses are corrupt or secondary. In those cases, the original or preferable reading is no longer attested in any extant manuscript but is fairly certainly established due to the textual evidence that remains.[10] And if we succeed in creating such a critical edition, we can trust that it will get us closer to the revelation at Sinai.

In sum, the biblical evidence from the Second Temple period, now available in the manuscripts from Qumran and long since available in the ancient versions, helps us see that the text bequeathed to us by the Massoretes is generally faithful to the ancient text but stands in need of correction in some details. The ancient text has been added to, changed, and subtracted from; in part the Massoretic text has "improved" upon the ancient text, and in part it has produced errors in the ancient text.

THE WORK OF THE MASSORETES

The Massoretic system of vocalization and accentuation (טעמים) described by Sanders is in fact a medieval system. Tiberian Massoretes devised and applied it between the sixth and ninth centuries. Their apparent intention was to fix the pronunciation, and in some cases the interpretation, of the traditional text as it had been handed down from ancient times. But we must admit that we have little control in determining whether that intention succeeded in its purpose or (like Origen's magnificent failure, the Hexapla) only partially succeeded and partially failed. We know that their efforts largely

---

10. We should recall that Wellhausen proposed emendations to the Massoretic text even though those Hebrew forms were not preserved in any manuscript in his day, and that some of these conjectural emendations have since turned up in biblical manuscripts at Qumran.

succeeded in preserving one form of the consonantal text of each book as it existed in the Second Temple period. But we also know that there were several competing systems of vocalization and accentuation (and thus interpretation)—not only Babylonian, Palestinian, and Tiberian systems, but also competing views within the Tiberian system itself, which emerged as dominant.

So even if the Massoretes achieved perfect success, what they have preserved is only one form among several accepted forms of the ancient text. And there are other forms (attested at Qumran, in the Septuagint, in the Peshitta, etc.) which at times certainly provide us with chronologically earlier and textually superior readings.

Consideration of the Massoretic critical apparatus, known as the Massorah Magna (מסורה גדולה) and Massorah Parva (מסורה קטנה), might clarify this chronological factor. A profound respect for the accomplishments of the Massoretic apparatus is, of course, warranted; but at times this might deflect scholars from a proper text-critical perspective—if by proper text-critical perspective one means seeking the best text, not necessarily the best form within the Massoretic tradition. In *From Sacred Story to Sacred Text*, for example, Sanders writes that in the Massorah Parva the ל signaling a *hapax* "stands like a soldier to remind the next scribe that the word in question must be copied precisely as written or corrected in the *Vorlage*," (and similarly for the אׁ signalling a psalmic hallelujah, and so forth).[11] But though these may have aided the medieval fidelity of the text, they may be entirely irrelevant for the ancient text (i.e., for Phase 2) because there was significant, if smaller scaled, change after the stabilization of the text and before the Massorot were

11. Sanders, *From Sacred Story to Sacred Text*, 137.

created. Thus, the Massorah Parva is indeed a "sentinel" to guard the medieval Massoretic text; but it may also be a decoy, albeit well intentioned, guarding a secondary, medieval variant, and distracting us from the *original*, *final*, or *canonical* reading.

Let me cite an example. Sanders says: "Often one can find in the Septuagint or the Syriac a variant that the Massorah warns the next scribe to be cautious not to emulate."[12] Now there are two possibilities: the original text could be either the Massoretic text reading or the Septuagint/Syriac reading. If the object is to find the *best* text, then virtually all textual critics—and our communities—would prefer the same version: either the Massoretic text reading *if* the Septuagint/Syriac has corrupted a late first-century reading; or the Septuagint/Syriac reading *if* the developing Massoretic text had later corrupted an ancient proto-Massoretic reading which had been faithfully translated by the Septuagint/Syriac. In either case, the Massorah does indeed warn us not to change the (medieval) Massoretic reading; but I suspect that, given the latter situation, most would agree that the text-critical scholar (of both the urtext and the canonical text variety) should adopt the Septuagint/Syriac reading. Similarly, if a reading was handed down correctly through the end of the ancient period but was copied incorrectly sometime long after Moses but before the Massoretes, our communities deserve the restored original text. Individual variants from Qumran manuscripts or the Septuagint may or may not get us closer to our text-critical goal; but analogously, medieval readings carefully guarded by the Massoretic apparatus may or may not get us closer to our goal, especially if the Massoretic reading is corrupt—albeit well guarded.

12. Sanders, *From Sacred Story to Sacred Text*, 137.

THE TEXT TO BE TRANSLATED

Another troublesome question is, What specific form of the text should be selected for Bible translations? *Massoretic text* is not a univocal term. That is, the Massoretic text is an anthology of canonical books, and the textual character of certain individual books is quite different from the textual character of others. We find different stages in the editorial process (or in the series of editions) of a given book, different degrees of superiority of textual forms, different degrees of corruption in the text (e.g., Genesis or Exodus as against Samuel or Hosea).

If we were to survey the multiple textual forms extant and attempt to devise criteria for determining which edition of the textual form of the biblical books we ought to isolate and translate (i.e., the earliest form, or the latest form, or whatever), by almost any text-critical criterion we would find ourselves translating the Massoretic text for one book, the Septuagint for another book, and perhaps a Qumran text for a third book. And sometimes we would even have to change textual forms within a specific book—because our manuscripts change in the middle of certain books (cf., e.g., the relationship of the Massoretic text vis-à-vis the Septuagint for 1 Samuel chapter 1 as opposed to that relationship for 1 Samuel chapters 17–18).[13] This is to say nothing of the minor, independent variants in individual verses.

Two possible conclusions emerge. The first applies insofar as we seek an edition of the Bible that translates a single textual form. I have argued elsewhere for the validity of producing a translation of the Massoretic text as it has been received,[14] but

13. For more detailed examples and more complete discussion of this issue see Ulrich, "Double Literary Editions," 101-16.
14. Ulrich, "Double Literary Editions," 111-13.

that is a different decision from producing a translation of the best text available. It would seem to follow from the point made in the previous section that, if we do have forms of the ancient biblical text that preserve *Tanakh* more faithfully, our communities deserve to have a translation of the more faithful formulation of the text. The second applies insofar as we seek an edition of the Bible that mirrors the dynamic nature of the growth of the biblical text at the hands of the believing communities in antiquity who faithfully handed it on but creatively augmented it and adapted it to contemporary concerns. Here I would endorse Sanders's vision of a pluriform translation that displays "the pluriformity we truly inherit."[15] This leads us to our final point, the so-called canonical text.

THE SO-CALLED CANONICAL TEXT

I submit that, precisely speaking, there is no such thing as "the canonical text." Brevard Childs has contributed to the pro-liferation of the use of this term, but it is an imprecise term. Childs himself states at one point that "there is no extant canonical text,"[16] but he nonetheless continues to use the term and even has a section of his Introduction with that term in the title.[17] The term *canonical text*, however, is an abbreviation for *the textual form of a canonical book or collection of books*. The difference is important; to clarify this a few words about *canon* are in order.

Canon is a technical term in theology with a fairly precise definition, and we ought to use it in its strict sense in theologi-cal discourse, as we would any technical term. If we sometimes

---

15. See Sanders's essay in this volume, "Hebrew Bible *and* Old Testament: Textual Criticism in Service of Biblical Studies."
16. Childs, *Introduction to the Old Testament*, 100.
17. Childs, *Introduction to the Old Testament*, chapter 4.6.

use the term strictly and sometimes use it loosely, then we invite confusing or erroneous conclusions. The technical use of canon represents a reflexive judgment, denotes a closed list, and in both Jewish and Christian tradition concerns biblical *books*, not the textual form of the biblical books.[18] Thus, though we have sacred books functioning as authoritative in antiquity, we do not have a canon in either Judaism or Christianity prior to the end of the first century C.E. To my knowledge, there is no evidence prior to the end of the first century either in Judaism or in Christianity to suggest that there was a reflexive judgment which resulted either in a fixed list of books or a fortiori in a fixed text either of individual books or of a unified collection of books.[19]

From the point of view of Christian use of the Old Testament, I would raise the question whether the process of stabilization of the rabbinic text (i.e., the consonantal form witnessed by the Massoretic text) did not happen after Christianity had emerged as a separate party or religious group. Phrased perhaps too baldly, Is it not true to say that the stabilization of the text of the Hebrew Bible happened too late for definitive use in Christian theology? Is there firm evidence for a canon, strictly speaking, in either Judaism or Christianity (much less a canon common to Judaism and Christianity) prior to the late

---

18. Sanders is aware of this usage but does not accept it (*From Sacred Story to Sacred Text*, 158). It seems to me, however, that his concern is centered on the Scriptures' *authoritative* function in the community, not on canon as such. The *norma normans*, or function of the canon, is indeed to be related to the canon—eventually, but not until we actually have a canon; prior to the conditions necessary for a canon as such, *norma normans* is more properly to be seen as a function of the authoritative books.

19. Ulrich, "Canonical Process." Beckwith's *Old Testament Canon*, which forces the canon much earlier, must be applauded for the great amount of data collected, but also used with caution because of the permeating deficiency in judgment and evaluative assessment of the data.

first century, prior to the self-conscious split between Judaism and Christianity? If we distinguish properly between authoritative books and the canon of books, we can see that both communities held certain books as authoritative, but neither group had yet made the reflexive or self-conscious decision that this collection of books and only the books in this collection are constitutive and authoritative always and everywhere for members of our community. That question was still being debated in later centuries. Thus, we had *authoritative* books, but we did not yet have a canon. Authoritative books *function* the same way (*norma normans*) as canonical books. But prior to at least the second century it is anachronistic and confusing to speak of a canon; we can, by contrast, speak of the canonical process, because that process by which the authoritative books functioned and eventually were judged to be constitutive had long since been at work.

Again, even Childs states that there is no extant canonical text. But if we remember the distinctions between empirical study and dogmatic position, and between official canon and functional canon, then, as I suggested earlier, even the canon need not be a stumbling block for Jews and Christians. In fact, one of the givens of modern theological scholarship is that Jews and Christians must and do take seriously the Hebrew Bible. Serious students in either tradition must also know and study the religious literature that surrounds and sheds light on the rabbinic Bible or the Old Testament. And most of us know that the rank and file of our own tradition mediate the content of the Hebrew Bible through one or other functional canon: the New Testament or the rabbinic corpus.

CONCLUSIONS

I have argued for a new perspective on the text of the Bible which Jews and Christians hold in common, a new perspective that takes into account the empirical evidence fortunately placed at our disposal by the discovery of the biblical manuscripts from Qumran. We have by no means solved the issue of *the original text*, but I have shown that the Massoretic text is not to be equated straightforwardly with that term in any of its senses; simply put, we now have the resources to do better at transmitting the ancient word at certain points than the Massoretic text does. We may applaud the work of the Massoretes; we have seen, however, that their work, while guarding "the words of Moses," does not uniformly guard the best wording of that message, but rather at certain points guards a later, improved formulation or an erroneous formulation. Finally, I have argued for greater precision in using *canon*, both in terms of books of the Bible rather than textual form of those books, and in terms of a closed list of authoritative scriptural books by conscious decision rather than merely of an open collection of authoritative books.

I could understand an objection that I have argued for an abandonment of the Massoretic text, but that would be inaccurate. The Massoretic text is a good, time-honored, textual tradition, and in fact the best, single textual witness to the Hebrew Bible we have. But it is now no longer the best we can provide. Only in this limited sense, then, do I suggest an *improvement* on the Massoretic text. For the New Testament we have in fact supplanted the *textus receptus* with a critically established text, and Christianity is probably better off and closer to the truth.[20] Similarly, the Roman Catholic church since the Council of Trent in 1545-63 had held that "if anyone does not accept these books as sacred and canonical. . . and as they are in the ancient Latin Vulgate . . . , let him be anathema."[21] Yet the Roman

---

20. See Colwell, *Best New Testament*.
21. Clarkson et al., eds., *Documents of the Church*, 46.

Catholic church officially abandoned the Vulgate almost fifty years ago,[22] and I know of no biblical scholar who doubts either that we now have a better formulation of the scriptures or that the church's appreciation of the scriptures has grown substantially.

If some are of the opinion that it is permissible for scholars to speculate in our studies but not in our Bibles or synagogues or churches, I would argue that is unfair and dangerous to keep the truth from our communities. We do, of course, need to develop the pedagogical resources and pastoral skills to mediate the truth to our communities. But if we are convinced of the conclusions of our seasoned scholarly study, do we have the right to keep the truth from our communities?

In closing, I would like to suggest that, if we can keep aware of the distinctions between empirical and dogmatic approaches to our study, between reasonably objective judgments and judgments made on subjective convictions; if we can grant that subjective convictions are legitimate and indeed important for us as individuals, as religious communities, as a culture, and as a global population; if we dare to adopt a stance of monotheizing pluriformity, as Sanders suggests, at least pretending that God is one: then our joint study can continue to be mutually illuminating and enriching, both to the world of scholarship and to the Jewish and Christian communities who look to us for intellectual and spiritual leadership.

---

22. While still using it, of course, as a secondary textual resource.

Part Two

The Theological Costs
of Historical Critical Study

Toward a Common Jewish-Christian Reading of the Hebrew Bible

ROLF RENDTORFF

Recently, Jon D. Levenson published an article entitled "Why Jews Are Not Interested in Biblical Theology."[1] Having read his article, one can only agree with him. If biblical theology really is as Levenson has portrayed it, there would indeed be no reason why Jews should be interested in it. And there can be no doubt that there is a lot of truth in his depiction of Christian biblical theology past and present. However, the reader is left with a question as to whether this really could be the last word on the issue. He or she wonders whether it would not be more apt to say that Jews are not interested in *Christian* (in particular Protestant) biblical theology because of its biases and because of "the failure of the biblical theologians to recognize the limitation of the context of their enterprise."[2]

Levenson's readers were soon rescued from uncertainty. Only one year after his article had appeared, he published a book that could hardly be deemed anything other than a piece of biblical theology, of *Jewish* biblical theology, of course. The

---

1. Levenson, "Why Jews Are Not Interested ," 281-307.
2. Levenson, "Why Jews Are Not Interested," 304.

author puts it clearly in the preface that one of the main motivations for him to write this book was "the lack of sophisticated theological reflection upon even such central and overworked aspects of the religion of Israel as creation and covenant," and that the book is to be understood as "a theological study."[3] This teaches us that not being interested in biblical theology does not mean, or at least need not mean, not being interested in a theological interpretation of biblical texts.

So we can leave aside the question of biblical theology as an established theological discipline and turn to the more general and more fundamental question of a theological reading of the Hebrew Bible. Because our main topic is the common reading of the Bible, let us try to find out what the aim of such a venture could be, what possibilities and chances we can ascertain to carry it out, what obstacles we will have to face, and how we can hope to overcome them.

Before doing so, it would be useful to realize that in many fields of Old Testament scholarship (here I consciously use the internationally established term Old Testament) there exists a seemingly unproblematic cooperation between Jewish and Christian scholars. The more remote the fields of research are from theological or even religious problems, the easier the cooperation seems to be. Yet it would be interesting to inspect the different fields of biblical research in order to find out how unproblematic the cooperation really is.

Let me give a few examples. Archeology is one of the preferred fields of cooperation between Jews and Christians. The evolution of methods and techniques is to a high degree a common endeavor. Of course, there is a certain competition and rivalry between different schools, yet in many cases this is not mainly an issue between Christians and Jews but rather, for

3. Levenson, *Creation and the Persistence of Evil*, xiv.

example, between conservatives and liberals, or however one wants to define the different groups or schools. Here the frontiers often cut across religious affiliations. To a certain degree this is also true with regard to the interpretation of the findings. But because this is linked with more general historical views, including the history of religion, at a certain point specific Jewish interests inevitably are at stake. I need only mention the far-reaching problems we now face with regard to the early history of Israel: the questions of nomadism, conquest, social revolt; the question of the origins of Yahwistic monotheism, and the like. All these problems have their implications for Israelite, and that means finally Jewish, historical identity. Conversely, Christian identity is not directly affected by these problems. The question is, To what degree are scholars conscious of those implications or motivated by more or less unconscious preconceived opinions?

I choose another example from the field of philology or linguistics. Learned Jewish biblical scholars now utilize sophisticated means to try to prove that P, the so-called Priestly Code, is of preexilic origin.[4] This appears to be a purely linguistic or even historical question. But obviously the discussion is motivated by the old and enduring fight against Julius Wellhausen's notion of the decline of ancient Israelite culture marked by priestly leadership. The interesting fact is that Wellhausen openly and explicitly used his arguments as anti-Jewish weapons; the modern linguists, by contrast, pretend, surely bona fide, to have purely scholarly interests. In my view it would be much more useful to discuss problems related to Wellhausen's views and those of his successors on postexilic Israel in their complexity and with an open and clear explanation of the interests involved.

4. I refer to Hurvitz, *Linguistic Study*, and several articles by the same author.

The third field I want to mention is the modern literary approach to the Hebrew Bible. Here we find Jewish and Christian biblical scholars working along the same lines, sometimes in explicit dissociation from the traditional *Literarkritik* (source criticism and the like), but mainly without mentioning those previously commonly accepted methods at all. In my view, in this field there are the fewest differences between Jewish and Christian scholars. But at the same time, many of those working in this field are not interested in theology but explicitly claim their method of interpretation to be purely literary. I appreciate this seemingly unbiased cooperation, but I do not believe that this will be very helpful for a theological understanding of the Hebrew Bible.[5]

Finally, if one examines the programs of international Bible congresses one finds very few contributions that could be deemed to be theological in a strict sense. Obviously there is something like a "historicist evasion," to use the term coined by Levenson.[6]

THE NECESSITY OF A COMMON BIBLICAL THEOLOGY

Let me return to the question of the rationale behind the endeavor for a common theological reading of the Bible by Jews and Christians. My first step toward an answer is to declare that in my opinion a common reading is an irrefutable necessity. The simple fact is that for both Jews and Christians the Hebrew Bible or Old Testament is Holy Scripture. If each group lived separated from the other in a world without any relation to the

5. With regard to the specific situation in North America with its "recent emergence of scholars and academic departments that are not beholden to any religious perspective," see Levenson, "Hebrew Bible, the Old Testament, and Historical Criticism," 52.

6. See Jon D. Levenson's essay in this volume, "Theological Consensus or Historicist Evasion? Jews and Christians in Biblical Studies."

world of the other, there would be no necessity to take note of different readings and interpretations of the respective Holy Scriptures. But this is not the case. On the contrary, since the very beginning of a separate history of Christians and Jews, that is, since the emergence of Christianity out of Judaism, both communities have been closely and, it seems, insolubly linked to each other, for better or for worse. This makes it virtually impossible simply to ignore the use of the Bible as made by the other religious community.

Since the fourth century C.E. the situation was determined by Christian dominance over the Jews. Therefore, the Christian interpretation of the then so-called Old Testament was the officially accepted one. There was no chance for a mutual exchange of views and opinions, and most Christians never heard about Jewish interpretation of the Bible, except from polemics and mostly incorrect details that were used for anti-Jewish purposes. I suspect that on the Jewish side, the knowledge of Christian interpretation of the Bible was not much better and not unbiased. This situation did not change substantially until the last century when after the enlightenment and the emancipation the Jews in Europe began to live under less oppression and to participate to some degree in the life of their Christian environment.

But even then, there was no real exchange between Jewish and Christian interpretations of the Bible. The reasons are manifold. First of all, Jewish and Christian communities lived without enjoying any relationship to each other and mainly without taking note of each other at all. Second, in the academic area, Jews had no access to the field of biblical studies because it was the domain of confessional Christian theological faculties.[7] Third, theology as a discipline generally was

7. See Goshen-Gottstein, "Christianity, Judaism, and Modern Bible Study," 69-88.

understood as something particularly Christian, and this view
was shared by many, if not most, Jews as well. Thus on both
sides, even those who were interested in a certain exchange
were convinced that there existed no Jewish equivalent to
Christian theology.[8]

One could argue that this situation perdures even until
today, and, generally speaking, this might be true. But the mere
fact of symposia and meetings, as well as several publications by
Jewish and Christian authors within the last few years, indicate
a change, or at least the beginning of something new.[9] It is the
first time in history that Jews and Christians have had the
opportunity to meet on an equal level, without being
dependent on any political or religious institution or authority,
and to meet as individuals, each with his or her own
commitment to a religious tradition and community. I have to
add, that, regrettably, this only became possible after the *Shoah*
(the Holocaust), and only forty years after that event. (Perhaps
this has something to do with the forty years mentioned
several times in the Bible.)

THE RELEVANCE OF JEWISH INTERPRETATION

The immediate question is whether we are ready and able to
begin a dialogue that should have started almost two thousand
years ago but now starts under fundamentally different
conditions. I believe that we have no alternative. As a
Christian, I want to say that it is high time for Christians to
begin to appreciate the Jewish interpretation of our common

8. Levenson tells the story of a continental biblicist who was unable in Israel
to find anyone interested in Old Testament theology ("Why Jews Are Not
Interested," 281).

9. I refer in particular to a symposium held in Bern, Switzerland, in January,
1985. The papers are published in Klopfenstein, Luz, Talmon, and Tov, *Mitte
der Schrift*.

Bible. The main precondition, from the outset, is to refrain from taking traditional Christian interpretation as a measurement for the meaning and relevance of Jewish interpretation.

Let me try to analyze the implications of such a claim. With regard to the Hebrew Bible or Old Testament, the first precondition is the theological acknowledgment of the fact that this book is the Holy Scripture of the Jews. Of course, historically speaking this is a mere truism. But as a Christian theological statement it is of fundamental importance. In Christian theological tradition, the Jews are usually spoken of in past tense with regard to the times of the Old and the New Testament. Jews of the present time are mainly subjects of political and social consideration. In the theological field, they figure first of all within the chapter on "mission." There is a great variety of opinions whether the Jews are just to be deemed as any other non-Christians (in Paul's words, "There is neither Jew nor Greek," Gal. 3:28), or as something special, perhaps still as God's elect people (according to another statement by Paul, "They are Israelites, and to them belong the sonship, the glory, the covenant" Rom. 9:4-5). In any case, the common Christian view of the Jews is that they should have acknowledged Jesus as the Messiah, and that there is still hope that one day they will do so (again according to a statement of Paul that at the and "all Israel will be saved," Rom. 11:26, which is interpreted [wrongly in my opinion] as the expectation of a final conversion of the Jewish people to Jesus Christ).

My claim to acknowledge, without any qualification, the fact that the Hebrew Bible is the Holy Scripture of the Jews presupposes the accceptance of the dignity and the independent value of the Jewish religion. This has a whole series of implications; and last but not least the question is at stake of the sole possession of the truth by the Christian Church, of the claim of the absoluteness of Christianity. I am fully aware of that, but I feel obliged to make it quite clear that in my opinion the first and foremost precondition for a serious and meaningful theological dialogue between Jewish and Christian biblical scholars is the theological acceptance of the Jewish religion on its own terms by its Christian partners.

In order not to be misunderstood, I have to add that this does not at all mean simply to turn things upside down and to claim Judaism to be the only legitimate successor of biblical Israel. The fact is that both Judaism *and* Christianity are successor religions of biblical Israel. Our task will be to acknowledge this fact and to define sensitively and clearly the theological meaning of this *and*. I believe that a responsible mutual discussion of our respective relations to the Hebrew Bible could be of great value for the definition of theological problems in general.

THE BIBLE AS A WHOLE AND IN PARTS

This leads to the problem of canon. Since the emergence of a new debate on the meaning of the canon of the Hebrew Bible or Old Testament, inaugurated particularly by Brevard Childs and James A. Sanders, a lot of literature on this topic has appeared.[10] I need not enter this discussion here; I confine myself to a few remarks. Whatever the history of the settling of the canon in its final form might have been, the fact is that both religious communities, Judaism and Christianity, have structured their religious traditions on the basis of the canon in its particular form, Hebrew or Greek. I do not believe it to be of great theological importance whether and when there was decision by any authority with regard to the canon, its content,

10. For the most recent discussion in Germany see Baldermann et al., *Zum Problem des biblischen Kanons.*

and its religious status, etc. From a certain time on, from the second or third century or whenever, both communities of faith took the collection of scriptures which we know now as the Hebrew or the Greek Bible as their Holy Scripture. That means that the number of books belonging to each collection as well as its wording was fixed at a certain time by decision or by custom. (Of course, I do not deny that the investigation of the history of canonization might be a very interesting scholarly field, but I doubt that the results will be able to contribute to the *theological* question of canon.)

This actual definition of the Bible as Holy Scripture implied a clear-cut distinction between the Bible itself and any other religious tradition, be it in writing or otherwise. Jewish tradition established a distinction between תורה שבכתב and תורה שבעל פה. On the one hand, this declares the Torah to be incomplete if not taken in both of its shapes; on the other hand, it does not allow us to mix them both up: הכתוב is only the Bible itself, and nothing else.

In Christianity's first stage, we find the same language. The New Testament regularly speaks of "the Scripture" (ἡ γραφή) or "the Scriptures" (αἱ γραφαί) when referring to the Jewish Scripture(s), Hebrew or Greek (which is itself a case of dispute among scholars). Later, another collection of books was added that eventually became the New Testament. Thus, from a certain point of view, the situation seems comparable with that in Judaism: the Bible, supplemented by other religious writings. But in fact the development unfolded very differently, especially in two respects. First, Christians took both collections together to be the one Bible. The original distinction between the two sets of books, and therefore the authoritative character of the original Scripture(s), had been given up. Canon or Bible was the whole two-part collection of holy writings. Second, within this Bible virtually only the New Testament had theological authority. The Old Testament was interpreted as supporting the New Testament, or as pointing toward it, or as a mere forerunner that sometimes did not see and understand things clearly enough. Of course, there were many hermeneutical variants through the centuries; but what is important in our present context is the fact that in the Christian tradition the Old Testament lost its independent value and authority, if not its independent meaning altogether.

THE REFORMATION AND MODERN CHRISTIAN THEOLOGY

If the denigration of Old Testament authority were still the state of affairs today, we would have no reason and no basis to discuss the topic of a common biblical theology. But it is not. In the meantime, two events took place that are related to each other in certain respects: the Reformation and the Enlightenment. It would go far beyond the scope of this paper to unfold the different aspects of these two fundamental events with regard to my topic, so I shall be very brief.

The Reformation brought to the consciousness of educated Christian people the existence of the Hebrew Old Testament as distinct from the Greek New Testament. At the same moment, at least at the margins of consciousness, the Jewish character of the Hebrew Bible appeared. (Luther himself was fully aware of that, with all the uneasiness that the insight caused him.) But first of all, a new awareness of the distinction and difference between the two parts of the Christian Bible arose. Therefore it was almost unavoidable that at the very moment when, two and one-half centuries later, the theologians of the Enlightenment began to discover the Bible as something in its own right (and not only as a source of *dicta probantia*, of prooftexts for dogmatics), they made a distinction between the two parts of the Christian Bible. The hour of birth for biblical theology[11] at the same time was the hour of birth for Old Testament theology as distinct from New Testament theology. At the same time, scholars realized the Jewish character of the Old Testament, or Hebrew Bible. Georg Lorenz Bauer equated "biblical theology of the Old Testament" with the "theory of the religion of the ancient Hebrews," which he also called the "history of Jewish dogmatics" (jüdische Dogmengeschichte).[12]

I think that this is the point in the history of the interpretation of the Bible whence our reflections should and could start. From then on, the Hebrew Bible has become a distinct and more or less independent subject of theological research. I say "more or less independent" because on the one hand Old Testament theology was declared to be the first part of a complete biblical theology, but on the other hand almost nobody actually wrote about both parts. The main interest was concentrated on the Old Testament; and only more than half a century later the first elaborated New Testament theology appeared.[13]

Yet with regard to our topic, one fundamental point did not change: the study of the Old Testament continued to be part and parcel of Christian theology. Therefore it shared the vicissitudes of theological trends and quarrels. During the nineteenth century Old Testament studies to a large extent lost its relationship to theology and turned toward becoming a purely historical and philological matter. But Old Testament studies always remained part of Christian tradition, even though disputed and denounced until the call raised by Adolf von

11. I refer to the famous lecture by Johann Philipp Gabler, "Oratio de justo discrimine theologiae biblicae et dogmaticae . . ." (1787).

12. Georg Lorenz Bauer, Theologie des Alten Testaments oder Abriß der religiösen Begriffe der alten Hebräer. Von den ältesten Zeiten bis auf den Anfang der christlichen Epoche. Zum Gebrauch akademischer Vorlesungen (1796).

13. Baur, Vorlesungen.

Harnack in 1921 for eliminating the Old Testament from the Christian church.[14] In any case, Christian theologians believed that they had to decide what to do with the Old Testament. And now I switch from past tense to present tense, because even today the situation remains unchanged for the majority of Christian theologians, in particular for Old Testament scholars: the Old Testament is, at least theologically speaking, only relevant, if not only existing, as part of the Christian tradition.

In the decades after the Second World War, Old Testament scholarship in Germany underwent a fundamental change toward a more explicit theological commitment, mainly as a consequence of the dialectical theology of Karl Barth and others, and intensified by the challenge of Nazi ideology, which compelled German theologians to defend the Old Testament as a legitimate component of Christian theology.[15] I believe that some of the present inconsistencies are based in the situation of the postwar years; since then many Old Testament scholars feel obliged to justify the use of the Old Testament within Christian church and theology, but they have never been educated for that undertaking. Therefore they try to do it with their own, homemade theological and hermeneutical instruments. I shall come back to this later.

SOME PROPOSITIONS FOR A COMMON BIBLICAL THEOLOGY

I claimed above that Christians, without any qualification, must acknowledge the fact that the Hebrew Bible is the Holy Scripture of the Jews. I added that this claim presupposes the

14. Harnack, *Marcion*.

15. For an insider it is, therefore, surprising to see Wellhausen (who explicitly denied being a theologian), Eichrodt, von Rad, and others (who explicitly wrote as Christian theologians) depicted as being in the same boat (see Levenson, "Hebrew Bible, the Old Testament, and Historical Criticism"), but the parallelism is indeed striking.

accceptance of the dignity, independence, and value of the Jewish religion. I am convinced that it is simple and evident that first of all Christian biblical scholars must realize and accept the fact that they are dealing with a book that is part and parcel of another living religious tradition as well, and that they must face the challenge to their traditional handling of the Old Testament.

Let me switch my usage once more, this time from the third person plural to the first person singular. From this point on, I want neither to attack nor to defend anyone. In other words, I want to leave the field of the history of Old Testament interpretation and research and enter the field of reflections on the possibilities and chances for a future common theological reading of our common Hebrew Bible. (I hope it will not merely be a path to Utopia.)

At the outset, let me state some of my presuppositions for the following remarks (without discussing or justifying them):

- The Hebrew Bible is a collection of Israelite (or Jewish) Scriptures which de facto obtained its final shape before either rabbinic Judaism or Christianity came into being. Therefore, neither a rabbinic nor a Christian interpretation of the Hebrew Bible can be historical.[16]
- For both (rabbinic) Jews and for Christians, the Hebrew Bible (or Greek Old Testament) is a fundamental basis for their religion but not the only base; for both religious communities, postbiblical traditions are of essential importance.
- In both traditions, methods of interpreting the Hebrew (or Greek) Bible have developed that are peculiar to the particular community and therefore cannot be claimed to be accepted by the other.

16. See Levenson, "Why Jews Are Not Interested," 286.

- Theological interpretation of the Hebrew Bible is not dependent on the theological system of the religious tradition to which the particular interpreter belongs: the Hebrew Bible is a theological book in its own right that can be, and must be, interpreted theologically from the inside.
- In doing so, the interpreter's theological approach unavoidably will be influenced by his or her own religious tradition; he or she should be conscious of this influence and should reflect on its hermeneutical consequences.
- Taking this into consideration, Jewish and Christian biblical scholars can work together toward a theological interpretation of the Hebrew Bible.

Let me try to unfold some of these points. One of the key points is the notion that the Hebrew Bible is a theological book on its own. That means that the Bible not only becomes theological by interpretation from a later elaborated theology, be it rabbinic or Christian; rather it would be possible and necessary to find the theological ideas and messages of the biblical texts themselves. At the same time, this implies that the authors of biblical texts are to be deemed to be theologians in a certain sense, who had theological ideas and purposes in mind when they spoke or wrote their texts, and even when they compiled the texts into larger units or books. This seems to be a truism. But if it is true, there would be no reason why Jewish and Christian scholars could not work together to explore the theological contents of biblical texts.

Several objections might be raised against such a concept: What is theology? Does it not have to be defined by each particular religious and theological tradition? This is an interesting question because the answer turns out to be circular. Certainly, each religious community developed its own system of theological questions and answers. But they did and still do so on the basis of the traditions that came down to them, including first of all the Hebrew Bible. So it would be an important trial to apply certain theological questions to the Hebrew Bible and to see whether they will prove to be adequate.

This could be one of the great advantages of a common theological reading of the Hebrew Bible by Jewish and Christian scholars. In some cases, it would turn out that discussions among biblical scholars would imply questions that also touch differences in the exegetical traditions of the two communities. Let me choose one example. The identity of the Servant of the Lord, the עבד יהוה, in Isaiah chapters 40-55 is disputed among Christian biblical scholars. Those who assume an individual understanding of the Servant could be open in principle to a christological interpretation; those who make no such assumption will be unable to take the traditional Christian interpretation as being in accordance with the meaning of the text itself. On the other hand, those who are inclined to a collective or corporate understanding could be open to the dominating Jewish interpretation of the Servant as representing Israel. The exegetical decision in most cases would be made, at least consciously, independently from the Christian liturgical and dogmatic tradition, but it will have far-reaching consequences for the hermeneutical relations between the scholar's own exegetical-theological insights and the Christian tradition of interpretation. Therefore it would be of high interest and value to discuss these different views with Jewish biblical scholars committed to their own religious tradition.

Another example could be the traditional Christian notion that to speak theologically about creation is only possible through Jesus Christ. One of the prooftexts for such a dogmatic position is Col. 1:15-17, where it is said that Jesus Christ is "the firstborn of all creation," and that "in him all things were

created, in heaven and on earth, visible and invisible."
Another text is, of course, John 1:1-3: "In the beginning was the
Word (ὁ λόγος), and the Word was with God, and the Word
was God. He was in the beginning with God; all things were
made through him, and without him was not anything made
that was made."

It is obvious and well known that this text reflects certain
hellenistic Jewish speculations about the חכמה in Prov. 8:22-31,
whose Greek equivalent is σοφία, which then was equated with
λόγος. A dogmatic notion built on those extrabiblical
speculations scarcely can serve as a hermeneutical key to a
biblical text. Outside Protestant Old Testament scholarship, this
dogmatic position is still widely held. But it is interesting to see
that in von Rad's commentary on Genesis there is no hint of
this Christian tradition. Westermann speaks in more general
terms about God's history with mankind that begins with
creation and finally has its center in what happend in Jesus
Christ, but he also does not mention the notion of creation
through Jesus Christ.

Yet both commentators, and others as well (for example,
Walther Zimmerli), mention the aspect of the seventh day of
creation and point to the relevance of the biblical Sabbath as
well as to certain eschatological aspects involved. But they are
not mentioning the importance of the Sabbath in postbiblical
and contemporary Judaism. Possibly they would argue that this
would go beyond the scope of their task as commentators on a
biblical text. But in any case, it would be interesting and useful
to discuss these things with Jewish biblical scholars. Then
Christian scholars would have to ask themselves what
consequences the shift from Sabbath to Sunday as the weekly
Christian holy day must have for the Christian interpretation
of Gen. 1:1-2:3, and whether it would be possible at all to

interpret the creation story without paying attention to the Jewish tradition of Sabbath.

At this point, I want to add a remark on the question, Why do Christian biblical scholars usually ignore or negate postbiblical Judaism? The answer seems to me to be simple: nobody told them that they should be interested in that tradition. There is no scholarly custom of dealing with Judaism; even now there is little literature by Jewish biblical scholars that would demonstrate the use of the postbiblical tradition; there is scant relevant scholarly literature that could introduce Christian scholars to the problems of dealing with Jewish exegetical tradition; there is a lack of translations of great parts of rabbinic literature, and so on. I fully understand the critical attitude of some Jewish scholars with regard to this deficiency, and I do not want to defend it; but I feel it is necessary to analyze carefully historical reasons before blaming individual scholars.

THE FUTURE OF COMMON BIBLICAL THEOLOGY

The two arbitrary examples just cited show that Christian biblical scholars in many cases are not eager to adapt their exegetical results to a certain Christian tradition. Rather, the contrary often is true. I believe that in the main Levenson is correct in saying that

> most Christians involved in the historical-criticism of the Hebrew Bible today seem to have ceased to want their work to be considered distinctively Christian. They do the essential philological, historical, and archeological work without concern for the larger constructive issues or for the theological implications of their labors. They are Christians everywhere except in the

classroom and at the writing-table, where they are simply honest historians striving for an unbiased view of the past.[17]

This is one side of the coin. The other side (castigated by Levenson very sharply as being inconsistent, if not insincere) is the attempt nevertheless to interpret the Old Testament as part of Christian theology. I tried to explain some of the reasons for this attitude, and I tried to formulate my own view of how to change this situation. I agree with Levenson that the crucial point would be the theological acceptance, or, first of all, even the awareness, of the existence of contemporary Judaism as a living religion using the Hebrew Bible as its Holy Scripture. Christian theologians, including Old Testament scholars, never have been taught to realize that. I myself during more then one decade of teaching Old Testament did not realize this problem at all. Only through several visits to Israel and through personal acquaintance with Jewish biblical scholars in Israel and the United States did I gradually begin to understand the whole problem, and I still feel I am at the beginning of discerning the consequences of these insights. As far as I can see, there are still very few Christian biblical scholars who are aware of all that.

One of the main obstacles to progress in this field is the fact that there is almost no exchange between Jewish and Christan biblical scholars on theological questions involved in the biblical texts. At the same time, there is an increasing debate on the so-called hermeneutical questions of how to understand the Old Testament within the framework of Christian theology, and whether and how to write a biblical theology embracing both parts of the Christian Bible. Levenson quoted from several books on Old Testament theology to demonstrate the obvious inconsistencies. The remarkable fact is that this kind of Christianizing interpretation is mainly, if not almost

17. Levenson, "Hebrew Bible, the Old Testament, and Historical Criticism," 49.

exclusively, to be found in this genre of books that try to embrace the Old Testament as a whole,[18] or in articles dealing with this problem, whereas in the commentaries on specific biblical books this kind of question is rarely raised at all.

What has to be done? In my view, the main point would be that Jewish and Christian biblical scholars who feel challenged by the current situation need to make efforts to bring to the awareness of Christian biblical scholars the crucial relevance of contemporary Judaism for any theological interpretation of the Hebrew Bible. This needs to be presented, of course, not with the attitude of imposing an absolute alternative, as if Christian scholars had to give up their present exegetical methods and take over Jewish exegesis. What would be necessary is to overcome the dichotomy that even now is used by Christians only one way. There are *two* traditions of reading and interpreting the Hebrew Bible. Neither has a monopoly; neither is to be neglected or even excluded.

In my view, the only promising way forward would be to work together on biblical texts or certain biblical topics or themes, instead of discussing general hermeneutical questions of how to relate Jewish and Christian views of the Hebrew Bible to each other. One day in the future it might be useful, and hopefully possible, to do this as well, but in my view it would be a fundamental mistake to begin with it.

Working on texts means asking for their theological meaning and relevance; the same is true for dealing with certain topics or themes. In his characterization of the general attitude of Christian biblical scholars, Levenson said: "They do the essential philological, historical, and archeological work without concern for the larger constructive issues or for the theological implications of their labors." Let us try to add to the

---

18. Perhaps Levenson is right to characterize this kind of book as Midrash (see "Hebrew Bible, the Old Testament, and Historical Criticism," 48).

essentials of their work the word *theological*, because a biblical text is never adequately interpreted without paying attention to its theological relevance, including the theological context of the text itself, of the chapter or book, and finally of the Hebrew Bible as a whole (here the discussion on canon and canonization becomes relevant).

Let me conclude with a quotation from the New Testament that seems fitting for our situation:

> When he saw the crowds, he had compassion for them, because they were harassed and helpless, like sheep without a shepherd. Then he said to his disciples. "The harvest is plentiful, but the laborers are few; pray therefore the Lord of the harvest to send laborers into his harvest" (Matt. 9:36-38).

Theological Consensus or Historicist Evasion? Jews and Christians in Biblical Studies

JON D. LEVENSON

When I first heard the theme of this volume—whether there can be a joint Jewish and Christian reading of the Hebrew Bible or whether we must choose between the *Tanakh* and the Old Testament—I immediately thought of the title of a collection that appeared a few years ago. The book is entitled *Biblical Studies: Meeting Ground of Jews and Christians.*[1] Now the idea that Jews and Christians might meet to discuss the Bible is hardly surprising. Consider, for example, the Great Disputation between Rabbi Moses ben Nachman and the convert Pablo Christiani in Barcelona in 1263. The difference, of course, is that the meeting that the editors intend is not marked by disputation but by its opposite, collaboration and cooperation. What has made this new situation possible is not only the phenomenon of ecumenical dialogue as it has developed over the past three decades, but also a change within biblical studies themselves, one that Lawrence Boadt is at pains to point out in his introduction:

---

1. Boadt, Croner, and Klenicki, *Biblical Studies.*

The tremendous gains in the study of Scripture itself in this century
. . . [mostly] stem from our vastly enlarged knowledge of ancient
history and civilization. This in turn has led to a deepened
understanding of the manner of expression and the literary output of
the semitic world, and has created a scientific passion for capturing
the original setting and sense of the biblical books.[2]

What this historical approach shows, according to Boadt, is that
"the relationship of the Hebrew Scriptures to the New
Testament . . . must begin with the premise that each speaks
from its own complete integrity."[3] Pablo Christiani, call your
office!

The idea that the historical study of the Bible has replaced
Jewish-Christian disputation with ecumenical collaboration is
not one with a resounding resonance among Jews. Solomon
Schechter, the great rabbinicist who was the guiding spirit of the
Jewish Theological Seminary of America in its formative
period, described "Higher Criticism" as "Higher Anti-
Semitism" and defined its goal as the destruction of the raison
d'être of the Jewish people, "denying all our claims for the past,
and leaving us without hope for the future."[4] And if this
polemic from the turn of the century seems out of date to you,
consider this scene from Chaim Potok's novel, *In the
Beginning* (1975). David Lurie, a yeshivah student on the verge
of ordination, has just informed his father Max of his
application to a biblical studies program in a university:

> "Tell me what it means to study Bible in a university. Your
> teachers will be *goyim*?"
> "And Jews."
> "The Jews are observers of the commandments?"
> "I don't know. They may be. I'm not certain."

2. Boadt, Croner, and Klenicki, *Biblical Studies*, 3-4.
3. Boadt, Croner, and Klenicki, *Biblical Studies*, 5.
4. Schechter, "Higher Criticism—Higher Anti-Semitism," 36-47.

"It is unimportant to you that they may not be observers of the commandments? . . . You will study Torah with *goyim* and with Jews who are like *goyim*? What do they know of the Torah?"[5]

It is easy to dismiss Max Lurie's words as the product of mere social prejudice, as tenacious as it is primitive, and simple fairness requires me to concede that such prejudice does indeed exist. I can attest from experience that in the minds of many Jews, perhaps most, and even many scholars of Judaica, it is better to study Bible with a Jew hostile to Jewish practice than with a gentile deeply respectful of it. Such irrationality, however, does not characterize David's father, for his concern is not that his son study simply with Jews, but with observant Jews and not, as he indelicately puts it, "with Jews who are like *goyim*." I find it fascinating that Boadt's introduction to the collection of essays never raises Max Lurie's question: in what way and to what degree are the Jews who meet Christians in biblical studies Jewish? Nor, I might add, does it raise the equally pressing converse of his question: What is Christian about the premise that Hebrew Scripture "speaks from its own complete integrity" over against the New Testament? If you will permit me to state in advance the conclusion of my paper, it is simply this: to the extent that Jews and Christians bracket their religious commitments in the pursuit of biblical studies, they meet not as Jews and Christians, but as something else, something not available in the days of Nachmanides and Pablo Christiani. The ground that the historical methods mentioned by Boadt have opened up can indeed be common to Jews and Christians, but more often it is neutral between them. Though Jews mindful of Barcelona in 1263 or of Schechter's "Higher Anti-Semitism" will be grateful for the small favor of neutral ground, neither they nor Christians should overlook the costs and the limits of religious neutrality. Nor should a method that

5. Chaim Potok, *In the Beginning*, 399.

studiously pursues neutrality be mistaken for the key to a genuine and profound dialogue between these two great religious communities.

ARGUMENTS FOR THE CHRISTIAN CHARACTER OF BIBLICAL STUDIES

Even this lesser claim that the modern study of the Bible takes place on ground neutral between Jews and Christians has been challenged. My colleague, James L. Kugel, has recently argued "that from its inception, this scholarly discipline was fundamentally a Protestant undertaking, one might even say, a form of Protestant piety" and one that "has, in ways great and small, still retained much of its particularly Protestant character." In support of his assertion, Kugel develops two types of arguments. The first is an argument from certain points often made by historical critics, "tantalizing particulars," as he puts it. The second and more profound argument involves the very stance of the modern critic, a stance that seeks "to establish as direct and unmediated a link as possible between the modern reader/interpreter and the biblical author at the moment of his speaking his words." This stance Kugel connects with the Protestant belief in a "flush encounter between man and God, unmediated by Church hierarchy and functionaries, by saints and human interveners."[6]

In his first type of argument, the "tantalizing particulars," Kugel offers what I regard as undeniable proof of a certain sort of Protestant bias in the putatively critical assessment of aspects of biblical history and thought. In the large amount of scholarly sympathy for the secession of the Northern Kingdom in the tenth century B.C.E., for example, Kugel, like myself,[7] sees a

6. Kugel, "Biblical Studies and Jewish Studies," 22.
7. Levenson, *Sinai and Zion*, 203-4, note 21.

retrojection of the Protestant Reformation itself. Jeroboam's "rejection of entrenched power (including a religious hierarchy)" and his establishment of relatively "decentralized worship" (with two royal chapels rather than one) is not, as the Deuteronomistic history would have it,[8] a sin of the highest order, but rather "a return to an older, truer . . . form of worship." Similarly, the relative lack of interest in the cult and the postexilic books bespeaks the classical Protestant preference for prophet over priest, for the word over the sacrament, and for the spirit over institutional structures, especially those that suggest the putative degeneration of Israelite religion into Judaism, that is, the religion that Jesus is thought to have hoped would be either cleansed or overthrown. Or again, Kugel notes that "among Semitic languages, there is one that has consistently been given the cold shoulder in Christian seminaries and secular universities: Mishnaic Hebrew," and he points out that the requirement of many Christian seminaries that New Testament students demonstrate knowledge of biblical Hebrew but not Mishnaic is odd, since it is the later dialect that is most relevant to their work.[9] These curricular decisions are obviously owing to a religious stance that is anything but neutral, as Kugel suggests. I might add that more than a few scholars who think, whether they acknowledge it or not, that rabbinic Hebrew and Aramaic are too distant to be relevant to the Hebrew of the Bible, still apply themselves vigorously to the study of Arabic that is half a millennium or more younger than these rabbinic tongues. And though no small amount of scholarly literature relevant to both Testaments of the Christian Bible is written in modern Hebrew, the number of scholars in this supposedly neutral field who can read modern Hebrew is exiguous. Only some form of residual

8. For example, 1 Kings 13:1-5.
9. Kugel, "Biblical Studies and Jewish Studies," 22.

Christian supersessionism can explain these strange, though all too familiar, data.[10]

Before considering Kugel's deeper argument, that the stance of critical scholars is essentially Protestant whatever their actual affiliation, I should like to add one particular of my own. This is the very definition of the field of biblical studies, even when the adjective refers only to the Hebrew Bible. The unspoken assumption of this definition is that the definitive break lies between the last of the biblical books (most likely, Daniel) and the next period, that of Qumran, Diaspora, and pre-Tannaitic Judaism, as well as of the nascent Church. I can imagine other ways of dividing the pie, though I cannot think of a program that actually does it so. Consider, for example, the tendency to speak of "Israelite religion" until the Exile but "Judaism" afterward. Though the distinction has traditionally been made in disparagement of the later period, a strong argument could be made that Ezra (fifth century B.C.E.), for example, has more in common with Rabbi Judah the Patriarch (late second–early third century C.E.) than either has with Isaiah of Jerusalem, the great prophet of the eighth century B.C.E. As the Jewish authorities in the Land of Israel acting under commissions from gentile emperors, Ezra and Judah faced similar challenges, challenges that were unknown to Isaiah, and they strove for similar goals, namely, the standardization of religious practice within a society whose penchant for tearing itself apart was potentially suicidal. Indeed, one might go further and draw a kind of typological parallel between the messianic fervor in Jerusalem two generations before Ezra (Haggai, Zechariah) and that in the same locale two generations before Judah (Simon bar Kosiba [= bar Kokhba]). Having done so, one could go on to

10. See Levenson, "Hebrew Bible in Colleges and Universities."

explore the legal activism of these two figures in light of this larger sociopolitical analogy between them.

My point is that the reason such studies are not common is that they are interdisciplinary, and this, in turn, is because the disciplinary boundaries have been drawn on grounds that are more confessional than historical. Every periodization makes a normative claim, though the claim is rarely explicit. The claim implicit in the setting of a disciplinary boundary between Ezra and Judah (but not between Isaiah and Ezra) is that a major revolution in the history of Judaism happened about the time of Jesus, so that biblical and rabbinic Judaism (admittedly different) cannot even be put on a continuum. In this connection, it is revealing to see how many studies entitled *History of Israel* end not with the last book of the Hebrew Bible, but two or three centuries later, in the time of the early church. A particularly curious and chilling example is Martin Noth's *History of Israel*, which ends after the defeat of the Bar Kosiba rebellion in 135 C.E. Noth's last sentence is this: "Thus ended the ghastly epilogue of Israel's history."[11] What is curious is that Noth had already conceded in his introduction that national sovereignty was not essential to his definition of Israel.[12] To be sure, he did regard the existence of a homeland and the "chance of united historical action," especially participation in a common cult, to be essential to "Israel."[13] The problem is that on the one hand, the Jews continued to live in their Palestinian homeland in large numbers for several centuries after 135 C.E., and on the other hand, the Diaspora had by that date already attained venerable antiquity anyway.

11. "Damit endete das schauerliche Nachspiel der Geschichte Israels": Noth, *Geschichte Israels*, 406; *History of Israel*, 454. (The first edition of Noth's book was issued in 1950.)

12. Noth, *History of Israel*, 4-5.

13. Noth, *History of Israel*, 7.

Furthermore, the rabbinic focus on the study and practice of Torah came to provide the sense of centrality and common experience that the Temple had offered in an earlier historical situation. Thus, Noth could just as easily have ended his history centuries earlier than 135 C.E., or centuries later. In fact, he could have acknowledged, like some other Christian historians of Israel (such as John Bright and J. Alberto Soggin), that the history of Israel has never ended and perdures to this day in the form of Jewish historical experience.[14]

So much for what is curious in Noth's conclusion. What is chilling in it is that only half a decade after the Holocaust, a German professor at the University of Bonn could write that "the ghastly epilogue of Israel's history" had happened eighteen hundred years before those horrific events. Obviously, Noth knew that the Jews continued to exist after the Hadrianic rebellion and were even establishing a state named Israel as he wrote his history.[15] His choice to terminate the history of Israel in 135 C.E.—though clothed in the garb of historical analysis— was actually motivated by theology: Jewry forfeited its status as Israel about the time that the last New Testament documents were being composed. This, in turn, reflects Christian supersessionist thinking, such as the insistence of Paul, or at least the early Paul, that it is Christians through faith rather than Jews through birth who inherit the status of Isaac, the son by the promise (Gal. 4:28-5:1). Noth's choice also reflects the hoary Christian idea that the destruction of the Temple and the dispersion of Jewry (which were not historically contemporaneous) were a punishment for the rejection of the

---

14. See Bright, *History of Israel*, 463-64; and Soggin, *History of Ancient Israel*, 336-37. It is still odd, however, that Soggin closes his book with a brief mention of the Diaspora, as if Jewry did not continue in the Land of Israel in large numbers for several centuries after 135 C.E., when his narrative ends.

15. Noth, *History of Israel*, 7.

claims made on behalf of Jesus. Here we must not fail to draw attention to Noth's remark that the failed rebellions against Rome culminated a "process of inner and outer dissolution." Presumably, the rabbinic religion that Jews have struggled for two millennia to uphold is a prime symptom of that putative process of dissolution. If we bear in mind that Noth and others like him sincerely presented themselves as critical historians rather than as theologians, is it any wonder that so many Jews consider historical criticism of their Bible to be not only *goyish* but anti-Jewish as well?

Kugel's second type of argument for the Protestant character of biblical scholarship, you will recall, involves not such "tantalizing particulars" as these, but rather the basic stance of the modern critic, a stance in which, in his words, "nothing was to intervene between the open page of the Bible and its interpreter."[16] It must not be missed that one can concede every one of the "tantalizing particulars" of Protestant or other Christian bias that Kugel and I (among others) have developed without conceding the larger and more profound point that the stance of devout Protestants and critical historians toward the text need be the same. The truth of a method must be logically distinguished from the uses to which it is put. At the end of the little essay of Kugel's from which I have been quoting, he does recognize this when he writes that "intellectual honesty compels [Jewish biblicists] to immerse ourselves in the disciplines of biblical scholarship and its conclusions (albeit . . . somewhat more on our own terms)." I take the assumption here to be that "the disciplines of biblical scholarship and its conclusions"[17] are not "in [their] very essence, Protestant"[18] after all—that is, that the Protestant conclusions are no more

---

16. Kugel, "Biblical Studies and Jewish Studies," 22.
17. Kugel, "Biblical Studies and Jewish Studies," 24.
18. Kugel, "Biblical Studies and Jewish Studies," 22.

necessary to the discipline of biblical studies than the
conclusions of Nazi eugenics, let us say, are necessary to the
discipline of genetics. The burden of the next part of my
argument is that the Protestant biases are not only unnecessary
to the historico-critical method, but, in fact, contradict its
assumptions. We begin by turning to the origins of historical
consciousness in the West.

PRE-REFORMATION HISTORICISM

In his study of *The Renaissance Sense of the Past*, Peter
Burke speaks of three elements that make up the "sense of
history": "the sense of anachronism," "the awareness of
evidence" (that is, a willingness to evaluate putative evidence),
and "the interest in causation." Lest his readers think that the
first element has always dominated the study of the past, Burke
points out that "medieval men lacked a sense of the past being
different in quality from the present."[19] As for the Bible,

> Since it was the word of God, who was eternal, there was no point
> in asking when the different parts of it were written down. It was
> treated not as a historical document but as an oracle; that is, what
> it had meant was subordinated to what it could mean.[20]

The lack of interest in authorship and literary chronology to
which Burke points is nicely exemplified by those medieval
Jewish exegetes who, like modern critics, doubted the inherited
doctrine of Moses' authorship of the entire Pentateuch, yet,
quite unlike modern critics, failed to consider the questions of
by whom and when the non-Mosaic passages were written. The
very medieval and very unmodern reason is nicely stated by
Joseph Bonfils (טוב עלם), a fourteenth-century rabbi who wrote
a supercommentary to Abraham ibn Ezra's Torah commentary:

19. Burke, *Renaissance Sense of the Past*, 1.
20. Burke, *Renaissance Sense of the Past*, 3.

"What should I care whether it was Moses or another prophet who wrote it, since the words of all of them are true and inspired?"[21] Some Jewish traditionalists, eager to show that modern biblical criticism is kosher, find in the heterodoxy of Ibn Ezra, Bonfils, and the like, the certificate of kashrut they are seeking,[22] but the last thing I can imagine modern biblical critics saying is that they could not care less who wrote a given passage. Indeed, nothing has been more characteristic of the modern study of the Bible than a passion for questions of authorship and dating, and this passion is the outgrowth of a certain very unmedieval skepticism about the divinity, eternity, and immutability of the biblical message. I might add that among those infected with this skepticism the central figures of the Protestant Reformation are not to be numbered.

It is in the time of Petrarch (1304-74) that Burke sees the beginnings of the change from the medieval to the Renaissance sense of the past. He points out that the great Italian poet "explored Roman ruins" in hopes of "reconstruct[ing] the past from its physical remains." He was, moreover, "interested in inscriptions," and "he collected Roman coins and used them as historical evidence."[23] Most important, whereas medieval lawyers "thought of law as something outside time," Petrarch insisted that law be seen in its historical context.[24] We need only remind ourselves that Petrarch and Bonfils were contemporaries to realize the difference between Renaissance

21. *Tsafenat Pacaneah* to Gen. 12:6. Since the book is not available to me, I translate this section from the citation of it in Greenberg, *On the Bible and Judaism*, 276.

22. For example, Sarna, "Modern Study of the Bible," 22-24; Greenspahn, "Biblical Scholars, Medieval and Modern," 245-58. On the conceptual flaws inherent in the effort to validate the distinctively modern study of the Bible by reference to medieval exegetical traditions, see Levenson, "Eighth Principle of Judaism," 208-13.

23. Burke, *Renaissance Sense of the Past*, 23-24.

24. Burke, *Renaissance Sense of the Past*, 5; 32-33.

and medieval thinking on this point and to become aware that the terms refer more to mentalities than to periods.

Petrarch's sense of anachronism led him easily to the second of Burke's three elements that make up the sense of history, "the awareness of evidence." Burke points out that arguing on both formal and substantive grounds, Petrarch was able to prove that a document purporting to exempt Austria from the domain of Emperor Charles IV was not written by Julius Caesar at all.[25] This foreshadowed a whole series of exposés of forgeries in the Renaissance, which, as I shall argue, is not unconnected to the emergence of modern biblical criticism. Burke points out that in the century after Petrarch, Nicholas of Cusa, Reginald Pecock, and Lorenzo Valla all independently exposed the *Donation of Constantine*, a document in which the emperor was supposed to have given temporal power over Italy to the popes.[26] This discrediting of an ecclesiastical charter in order to assist in the birth of a new political order also foreshadows the emergence of the historico-critical attitude to the Bible two centuries later, as we shall soon see.

Burke also takes note of Valla's *Annotations on the New Testament*, in which he thinks "of the Bible as a historical document, written in particular historical circumstances," and not an inalterable document either, as his willingness to suggest textual emendations shows. Burke connects this with the work of John Colet (c. 1467-1519), a friend of Erasmus who "compared [the New Testament] with other sources for ancient history," such as Suetonius's life of Claudius. But most relevant to the birth of biblical criticism is Cusanus's *Cribatio Alcoran* (*The Sieving of the Qur'an*; 1460) in which three components are distinguished, in Burke's words, "Nestorian Christianity, a

25. Burke, *Renaissance Sense of the Past*, 50-54.
26. Burke, *Renaissance Sense of the Past*, 55.

Jewish adviser of Muhammad, and the corruptions introduced by Jewish 'correctors' after Muhammad's death." "This was," as Burke notes, "to treat the Koran as a historical document, and to write the history of its leading ideas."[27] It would be two centuries until men like Benedict Spinoza and Richard Simon would approach the Bible in the same way, but the connections of the nascent historical criticism of the Bible with the Renaissance sense of the past are undeniable.

Every one of the figures I have named in this connection— Petrarch, Cusanus, Pecock, Valla, and Colet—lived before the Protestant Reformation. It is not the Reformation that originated the acute and potentially explosive awareness of the difference between primary and secondary meanings, between primary sources and their secondary elaboration or distortion. What the Reformation did was to recast this awareness in highly charged theological language (*sola fide, sola gratia, sola scriptura*) and, in some instances, to change the relative preference for original meanings, already rapidly growing less relative, into something more like an absolute norm. "The Scripture hath but one sense," proclaimed William Tyndale (c. 1492-1536), "which is the literal sense."[28] It must not be missed, however, that the tendency to set aside all senses but the basic (פשט in medieval Hebrew parlance) had been going on for over four centuries when the Reformation began. Moshe Greenberg points out that from the eleventh century on, Jewish exegesis is marked by "ever-increasing skill in, and preference for, ascertaining the plain sense . . . an awareness of the invalidity of midrashic interpretations as an exegetical resource," and by "a growing interest in the historical context of prophecies," as witnessed, for example, in the work of David Qimḥi (1160-

---

27. Burke, *Renaissance Sense of the Past*, 58-59.
28. Burke, *Renaissance Sense of the Past*, 61.

1235).[29] It does not strike me as coincidental that the great age of Midrash compilation was coming to an end just as this preference for Scripture's plain sense (פשט) over its homiletical meaning (דרש) was coming into its own. My point is that the awareness of the difference between primary and secondary meanings and the preference for the former for purposes of exegesis are not unique to Protestantism or even to Christianity, nor do they originate with the Renaissance sense of the past and its embarrassment at anachronism. It did not take the Reformation to teach Jews that the study of Midrash is not the study of *Tanakh*. What Protestantism introduced was a certain contempt for everything that was not biblical and a conviction that tradition that was not faithful to Scripture was illegitimate (though Protestantism here had a Jewish antecedent in Qaraism). To the extent that modern biblical studies takes those positions, it is indeed indebted to certain forms of Protestantism, but the history of biblical studies among Jews and Catholics abundantly demonstrates that the modern methods hardly require those classical Reformation attitudes.

SPINOZA, THE RENAISSANCE, AND SECULAR LIBERALISM

As I wrote above, Spinoza's work on the Bible, though it came in the middle of the seventeenth century, is best placed within the tradition of the new sense of the past of the Renaissance humanists. To be sure, at times Spinoza sounds Protestant and thus appears to lend credence to the claim that biblical criticism, of which all concede he was a pioneer, must follow a Protestant agenda. When, for example, he tells us that "our knowledge of Scripture must then be looked for in

---

29. Greenberg, "Exegesis," 215.

Scripture only,"[30] he echoes the Reformation claim that the Bible is its own interpreter (*interpres sui ipsius*) and requires no ecclesiastical or other traditionary mediation. And when he concludes that the "authority of the Hebrew high-priests [is not a] confirmation of the authority of the Roman pontiffs to interpret religion, [but] rather tend[s] to establish universal freedom of judgment,"[31] he echoes a Protestant note that goes well beyond the humanist critiques of the fifteenth century. This same penchant for breaking with traditional authority rather than simply protesting its misuse can be seen in Spinoza's treatment of Judaism. Excommunicated for obscure reasons from the Sephardic congregation of Amsterdam in 1656, Spinoza turned against the Jewish tradition and even against the Jews themselves with fury. "Now the Hebrew nation has lost all its grace and beauty," he wrote.[32] Their preservation is owing largely to "gentile hatred,"[33] their religion having already in the Second Commonwealth sunk "into a degrading superstition, while the true meaning and interpretation of the laws became corrupted."[34] Spinoza's anti-Judaism both recapitulates classical Christian supersessionism and adumbrates an important theme among scholars of Israelite history, and of Old Testament theology, into our own day. In fact, few scholarly models have been more enduring in any field than biblical studies' degenerative model of ancient Israelite history, with its ideal early period being progressively corrupted by Jewish priests and legists. The content of the ideal may change—most recently, it has become social and sexual

---

30. Spinoza, *Tractatus*, 100. The *Tractatus Theologico-Politicus* was originally published in 1670.

31. Spinoza, *Tractatus*, 119.

32. Spinoza, *Tractatus*, 108.

33. Spinoza, *Tractatus*, 55.

34. Spinoza, *Tractatus*, 238.

egalitarianism[35]—but the underlying model has proven phenomenally durable, and this is undoubtedly to be connected with the fact that a principal bête noire is somehow always *halakhic* Judaism.[36]

In spite of these patent debts to Protestant and generally Christian positions, Spinoza's biblical criticism is actually, at the level of fundamental method, profoundly at odds with the Christian legacy and especially with its Reformation component. To take the essential point first, Spinoza denied supernatural revelation altogether. In contrast to the Protestant doctrine of the Bible as the unique and unparalleled word of God, Spinoza held that since "our mind subjectively contains in itself and partakes of the nature of God . . . it follows that we may rightly assert the nature of the human mind . . . to be a primary cause of Divine revelation."[37] Spinoza writes here of "the human mind" and not the inspired mind because in his view revelation (if we may still use the old term to denote the new entity) was universally available, and the prophets differed from the masses only by virtue of their "unusually vivid imaginations"; they had no special knowledge.[38] Now if Spinoza's position looks like an escalation of Luther's notion of the priesthood of the universal believer (as it may in part be), consider that the claim of special authority that he sought to discredit was not simply that of the Church but that of the Bible itself. Spinoza's dagger is aimed at the very heart of the

35. See, for example, Gottwald, *The Tribes of YHWH*, passim.
36. See Levenson, "Hebrew Bible, the Old Testament, and Historical Criticism," 28-47. It is significant that some efforts to counter the anti-Jewish interpretation have to rely on the practice of nonrabbinic groups. See, e.g., Brooten, *Women Leaders*. The position she holds—that the desired values did indeed appear among Jews in late antiquity, that is, among those groups that the rabbinic movement supplanted—is no consolation to those Jews seeking to uphold the rabbinic tradition.
37. Spinoza, *Tractatus*, 14.
38. Spinoza, *Tractatus*, 27.

Protestant concept of authority, that is, the pneumatic experience that was thought to have produced the Bible and, through it, to animate the special life of Christians. When Spinoza concluded that "the rule for [biblical] interpretation should be nothing but the natural light of reason which is common to all—not any supernatural light nor any external authority,"[39] he was protesting Luther and Calvin no less than the Roman church. Earlier we saw that the humanist slogan "back to the sources" (*ad fontes*) set the stage for the Reformation doctrine of exclusive scriptural authority (*sola scriptura*). Now we see the movement come full circle, as Spinoza grants to the Bible no more reverence than the humanists granted the *Donation of Constantine* or than Cusanus granted the Qur'an. As Michael L. Morgan puts it, "Spinoza's hidden assumption is that the Bible is like any other book."[40] It is this humanistic, rationalistic assumption (for it is never really argued, but only presupposed) that separates Spinoza from the classical Jewish and Christian traditions. Though the assumption is one that may have caused him a certain social isolation in seventeenth century Holland, it is also one with a vast resonance in the subsequent history of biblical criticism. One need only consider that the idea of reading the Bible "like any other book" played a central role in the great manifesto for biblical criticism of Benjamin Jowett, "On the Interpretation of Scripture," published in 1860.[41] An assumption external to both Judaism and Christianity was put forth as the regulative principle for reading their respective foundational literatures.

39. Spinoza, *Tractatus*, 119.
40. Michael L. Morgan, "Scriptural Religion in Spinoza's *Tractatus Theologico-Politicus*" (draft manuscript graciously sent to me by the author), 16.
41. Jowett, "On the Interpretation of Scripture." See also Barr, "Jowett."

Given Spinoza's naturalism, it follows that the meaning of a scriptural passage is the author's meaning alone, not God's, or, as he put it, "we are at work not on the truth of passages, but solely on their meaning."[42] In order to find that out, we must engage in that activity which, as we saw, was so marginal to the medieval Jewish commentators, even those who doubted the traditional attributions: we must determine "the life, the conduct, and the studies of the author of each book, who he was, what was the occasion, and the epoch of his writing, whom did he write for, and in what language."[43] It is in Spinoza's program for biblical scholarship in Chapter VII of the *Tractatus Theologico-Politicus* that we see the origin of the preoccupation with dating and authorship that dominated the distinctly modern study of the Bible until this generation and continues to flourish. The effect has been the dismemberment of the Bible, as its components are disengaged from the larger whole and assigned to different periods, schools, and social sectors. The equivalent of the Christian sin against the Holy Spirit for this author-centered hermeneutic is "taking a passage out of context," the last word referring not to the *literary* context which is the larger Bible, Jewish, Catholic, or Protestant, but to the *historical* context of the original author, who was, of course, neither a rabbinic Jew, nor a Roman Catholic, nor a Protestant. The effect, whether intended or not (I believe Spinoza intended it), is to deny the Bible to traditional religion on biblical grounds, or as Morgan nicely puts it, to "proceed on the basis of the Bible to transcend the Bible."[44] If, as Schechter thought, higher criticism sought to destroy the raison d'être of the Jewish people, it must also be pointed out that if the critics had followed the program of Spinoza's great *Tractatus*, as in

42. Spinoza, *Tractatus*, 101.
43. Spinoza, *Tractatus*, 103.
44. Morgan, "Scriptural Religion," 1-2.

some measure they have, then the raison d'être of the Church would also be undermined, and on grounds that the churches could hardly reject—the message of the Bible itself!

Richard H. Popkin points out that Spinoza fits into a tradition of skepticism fueled in no small measure by the Reformation itself, which having denied "the fundamental criterion" of Christian authority, willy-nilly unleashed a great criteriological problem: "How does one tell which of the alternative possibilities ought to be accepted?"[45] But, as Popkin also notes, Spinoza's skepticism on religious matters did not extend to mathematics and metaphysics.[46] I would add that one result of this displacement of authority from religion to philosophy (with which Scripture was no longer to be harmonized) was a theoretical relativization of Judaism and Christianity. Leo Strauss hinted at this when he observed that for Spinoza, the two Testaments were equal, so that the characteristic features of each (such as Torah and commandments [מצוות] or the Cross) are dispensable because they cancel each other out.[47] Indeed, the reason, according to Spinoza, that critical investigations are essential is "that we may not confound precepts which are eternal with those which served only a temporary purpose."[48] What is left after these operations have been completed is a few vague moral imperatives, namely, the practice of justice and charity and obedience to the state.[49] These are the substance of the universal and immutable philosophical religion with which Spinoza hoped to replace Judaism and Christianity and thus to end the political turmoil and insane bloodletting that Christian

45. Popkin, *History of Skepticism*, 3.
46. Popkin, *History of Skepticism*, 299.
47. Strauss, *Spinoza's Critique of Religion*, 116, 120.
48. Spinoza, *Tractatus*, 103.
49. Spinoza, *Tractatus*, 9.

sectarianism had inflicted upon his country and the rest of Europe.

In order to put religious divisions behind him without attacking the Bible head-on, Spinoza had to show that the divisions in humanity that its law mandates—the divisons between Jew and gentile and between Christian and non-Christian—are now simply obsolete. Thus, he argues that the law revealed by God to Moses was merely the law of the ancient Hebrew state; therefore "it was binding on none but Hebrews, and not even on Hebrews after the downfall of their nation."[50] If this idea that the Torah once obligated only the Jews and now not even them looks like Pauline supersessionism, look again, for Spinoza argues not from dispensationalism, but from history; he sees no change of aeons, but only a new political situation. His assumption is that these putatively spiritual systems are really only political. Whereas Maimonides, for example, had seen the Mosaic polity as the correlative within politics of God's characteristic actions,[51] for Spinoza the issue was exclusively one of social control. (In this, he anticipated the ideology critique now so fashionable among liberationist exegetes and deconstructionist critics.) History supplied Spinoza with the coffin into which he placed the Torah. Again, an analogy with the Renaissance humanists and their discrediting of documents like the *Donation of Constantine* readily suggests itself. Today it is too easily forgotten that the context in which pioneers of biblical criticism like Spinoza and Thomas Hobbes[52] presented their heterodox findings was one of political debate in which the authors' goal was to free the political order from subservience to religion. The easiest way to accomplish this goal was to attach the religious documents inextricably to a

50. Spinoza, *Tractatus*, 8.
51. For example, *Guide to the Perplexed* 1:54.
52. See *Leviathan*, chapter 33.

vanished political order. Allow them to survive that past order and they might recreate it, as the Puritans were, in fact, seeking to do.

A contemporary described Spinoza as "a very poor Jew and not a better Christian";[53] a scholar of our day has connected Spinoza's relativization of Judaism and Christianity with his family's Marrano past. The Marranos, you will recall, were Iberian Jews who chose baptism into Roman Catholicism over the alternative of expulsion, yet continued secretly to practice some Jewish rites. "The clandestine character of worship, Catholic education, the lack of Jewish education, a mental mixture of both faiths, and isolation from the living Jewish communities outside Iberia," writes Yirmiyahu Yovel, "created with time a special phenomenon in the history and sociology of religion, a form of faith which is neither Christian nor actually Jewish."[54] The effect of this compounded marginality was often an unbearable sense of dissonance, one that could be most easily resolved only through the transcendence of *both* traditions. Indeed, listed among the Marrano patterns that Yovel finds in Spinoza are "heterodoxy and the transcendence of revealed religion," and "a skill for equivocation and dual language."[55] The first is nicely illustrated by Spinoza's disqualification of the characteristic features of each Testament, the chosenness of Israel, the Torah, and the commandments (מצוות) in the Old, and the incarnation of God and the redemptive death and resurrection of Jesus in the New. The second, the equivocal language, is also in plentiful evidence in the *Tractatus*, as when Spinoza defines *theocracy* as a regime with separation of powers, using a slogan of the Calvinist party

53. Feuer, *Spinoza and the Rise of Liberalism*, 143.
54. Yovel, "Marrano Patterns in Spinoza," 466. See also Feld, "Spinoza the Jew."
55. Yovel, "Marrano Patterns in Spinoza," 473.

in a sense that no Calvinist would have accepted[56]—that is, if he were careful and not hoodwinked by Spinoza's clever manipulation of traditional language for very untraditional purposes.

A more portentous example of this pattern of dissembling can be seen in Spinoza's account of why the Hebrew Commonwealth fell. Among the causes for this, according to him, were the priestly institutions (especially the tithes), prophecy (which he associated with fanaticism and subversion), and kingship (which he equated, at least in this tractate, with tyranny).[57] Now any student of the Hebrew Bible knows that priests, prophets, and kings all take it on the chin quite a bit in that book, and the very worth of all three institutions was questioned at times. But what Spinoza does not respect is the claim of the text itself that each of them was divinely ordained and the fact that, on balance, the Bible is positive about them all. Spinoza, to be sure, was not the first person to read the Bible selectively or to twist its sense to meet his needs. What he did pioneer, however, was the systematic transference of the normativity of the Bible from its *manifest text* to its *underlying history* (at least as he reconstructed it). In part, this, too, is a continuation of Renaissance humanism. Chapters 17 and 18 of the *Tracatatus Theologico-Politicus* resemble nothing so much as Machiavelli's accounts of how ancient kings and contemporary princes had lost their powers[58]—though, of course, Spinoza's substantive advice is very different from Machiavelli's. The Bible has become like any other political text, and its real meaning lies not in its textuality, but in its

56. Feuer, *Spinoza and the Rise of Liberalism*, 121.
57. Spinoza, *Tractatus*, chapters 17 and 18. See Feuer, *Spinoza and the Rise of Liberalsim*, 131-35.
58. E.g., Machiavelli, *The Prince and the Discourses; The Prince*, chapters 4 and 24.

historical message, of which its own authors may have been unaware. The *meaning* of the Bible belongs to the original author; the *message* of the Bible belongs to the contemporary moralizing historian. And when the message is derived from the underlying history and not from the manifest text that it often contradicts, then we are very much in the world of modern historical criticism and far indeed from the world of traditional religion, including the world of the Protestant Reformers.

The brunt of my argument to this point is that the results of the historical-critical study of the Hebrew Bible have rather generally been at odds with the underlying method. The method is historical and therefore privileges the period of composition at the expense of all later recontextualizations. The results have been skewed toward one of those recontextualizations, the Christian Church, as Christian categories, preferences, and priorities have been restated and even occasionally reenergized by historical critical study. The *method* derives from the Renaissance sense of the past as this is transformed through Enlightenment rationalism and then Romantic hermeneutics, with its emphasis on self-expression and authorial intention. The *results* are more than occasionally biased towards the Christian faith in the forms in which it already existed before the Renaissance, the Enlightenment, or Romanticism. The cause of this anomalous situation is to be found in the placement of biblical studies in church-sponsored institutions or in departments whose central concern is the study of Christianity: the method and its institutional location are at odds. A times, this has been recognized, as when the great historical critic Julius Wellhausen resigned his professorship in Greifswald on April 5, 1882. "I became a theologian because the scientific treatment of the Bible interested me," wrote Wellhausen in his letter of resignation:

Only gradually did I come to understand that a professor of theology also has the practical task of preparing the students for service in the Protestant Church, and that I am not adequate to this practical task, but that instead despite all caution on my own part I make my hearers unfit for their office. Since then my theological professorship has been weighing heavily on my conscience.[59]

Usually, however, the problem is covered over through compartmentalization. What the Bible *means now* and what it *meant in its own time* are sharply distinguished, as exegetes happily pass the former off to theologians (whom they nonetheless often accuse of taking the Bible out of context) or even deny that one can talk meaningfully about the Bible in any tense other than the past.[60] It is here that we confront the two-sidedness of historical inquiry. On the one hand, it can drive a wedge between the present and the past by showing how different they are. On the other hand, it can help retrieve the past for the present by reconstructing the missing context and thus adding essential resonance and verisimilitude. Historical criticism itself is neutral between these two opposing movements. It can help to heal—though not to reverse—the rupture caused by historical consciousness, or it can aggravate the rupture and help in dismantling tradition. To the extent that historical critics restrict themselves to descriptive history and avoid the thorny question of contemporary appropriation, they contribute, even if inadvertently, to the dismantling of tradition, rather than to the healing of the rupture. For historical criticism so restricted subtly fosters an image of the Bible as having once meant a great deal but now meaning little or nothing.

It has not, to my knowledge, been pointed out that this image corresponds to the biographical pattern of a large number

---

59. Quoted in Smend, "Wellhausen and his *Prolegomena*," 6.
60. See Ollenburger, "What Krister Stendahl Meant."

of contemporary biblical critics. These are people whose early lives were dominated by an intense religious commitment, in many cases fundamentalism, but whose adulthood is marked by quiet acculturation to the secular liberalism of the academic world and often by a slow but steady disaffection from all religious institutions. Among biblical scholars, even some of the most outspoken and effective debunkers of traditional religious views are—though you would never guess it—ex-clerics or graduates of theology departments.[61] Of course, the field is not lacking in scholars with active religious lives and congregational affiliations: not every Catholic in biblical studies is lapsed, not every Jew is nonobservant, and not every liberal Protestant values the adjective more than the noun. But even among those who practice, it is the past-tense sense of Scripture that still predominates. The remarkable pluralism of the field rests on a foundation of historicism, and the cooperation of diverse groups is purchased at the cost of the tacit denial on the part of all that the diversity ultimately matters. It is in the historico-critical study of the Hebrew Bible that what Yovel calls the "Marrano pattern[s]" achieve their most striking victory. Judaism and Christianity have become historical contingencies, relativized by historicism and replaced as indications of absolute truth not by philosophy but by the amorphous secular liberalism that dominates the academic world.

This brings me back to Boadt, and to Max Lurie in Potok's novel. Boadt tells us that one major reason that biblical studies have become a "meeting ground for Jews and Christians" is a new atmosphere of "scientific passion for capturing the original setting and sense of the biblical books." But Max Lurie asks whether the Jews who engage in this quest are observant or, as

61. See Smith, "Study of Religion," 132: "The courses actually available, and the training of men actually available to them, are on the whole calculated to turn a fundamentalist into a liberal."

he puts it, "like *goyim*."[62] I would explicate his question by asking: *is the price of this restoration of the past to the Bible not the relegation of the Bible to the past, so that the scholar's own practice or lack of it is of no relevance?* Is the fact that Jews and Christians can meet as equals in biblical studies owing to an unspoken agreement to treat the Scriptures of each community only according to the canons of historical relativism? If so, then the designation of those who so meet as "Jews" or as "Christians" is really only vestigial. If the Jewish scholars are "like *goyim*" and the Christian scholars are more scholarly than Christian, then the adherents of each community will wonder with Max Lurie whether this historical approach to the Bible is a net gain.

I repeat that I am convinced that the restoration of historical context to the Bible can help bring it alive and add vast depth and meaning to our study of it. The problem to which I am pointing is that much biblical scholarship is not practicing any such hermeneutic of retrieval. Instead, its operative technique is too often a trivializing antiquarianism, in which the bath water has become more important than the baby and the enormous historical and philological labors are not justified by reference to any larger structure of meaning. This antiquarianism is parasitical in that its place in the curriculum depends on a supracurricular commitment that it refuses to nourish and occasionally even belittles.[63] In theory, of course, it should be possible to affirm the meaningfulness of the Bible on secular grounds, and, in some ways, this is what the new

---

62. Boadt, Croner, and Klenicki, *Biblical Studies*, 3-4; Potok, *In the Beginning*, 399.

63. Cf. Steinmetz, "Superiority of Pre-Critical Exegesis," 38: "Until the historical-critical method becomes critical of its own theoretical foundations and develops a hermeneutical theory adequate to the nature of the text which it is interpreting, it will remain restricted—as it deserves to be—to the guild and the academy, where the question of truth can endlessly be deferred."

literary criticism of the Bible is doing. As we are about to see, however, the new agenda is itself more indebted to traditional theological positions than it cares to admit, and, in this, it carries on some of the worst defects of the antiquarianism that it so sternly opposes.

HEBREW BIBLE INSTEAD OF *TANAKH* OR OLD TESTAMENT

The subsequent history of biblical criticism has largely followed Spinoza's program of ascertaining "the life, the conduct, and the studies of the author of each book, who he was, what was the occasion, and the epoch of his writing, whom did he write for, and in what language [and] the fate of each book."[64] The birth of source criticism in the century after Spinoza and the emergence of Romanticism and the rediscovery of the ancient Near East in the next century brought about a focus on authorship that dwarfed Spinoza's own. Benjamin Jowett, in his controversial essay "On the Interpretation of Scripture" (1860), came to insist that "Scripture has one meaning—the meaning which it had to the mind of the Prophet or Evangelist who first uttered or wrote, to the hearers or readers who first received it."[65] Today, when so many scholars, especially in literature departments, are attacking biblical criticism for atomizing the Bible, it is salutary to recall the underlying purpose of source criticism—to restore passages to their historical context, to avoid anachronistic

---

64. Spinoza, *Tractatus*, 103. But what I call "trivializing antiquarianism" has forgotten Spinoza's purpose in this, "that we may not confound precepts which are eternal with those which serve a temporary purpose." Of course, the distinction was not hard to make for Spinoza, since those precepts that conformed to his philosophy (there weren't many) were simply presumed to be eternal and those that did not, to be historically contingent. This has remained the method of religious liberals to this day, and it accounts in no small measure for the relative lack of interest in Scripture in liberal communities.

65. Jowett, "On the Interpretation of Scripture," 36.

interpretation, and to recover the sense of the growth and dynamism of the biblical tradition which redaction and canonization have suppressed. The fact that Jowett's essay was published only one year after Charles Darwin's *On the Origin of Species* (1859) and in the same country suggests a fruitful analogy: the contiguity in the Bible of two passages from very different periods is as profoundly misleading as the presence in the same pit of the bones of both dinosaurs and humans. The dismemberment of the Bible and the reassignment of its parts to more original documents or life settings are necessary implications of historical thinking. To fail to do these things would be to fail to reckon adequately with the historical context.

The problem is that by making the *historical* context sovereign and regulative, historical criticism destroys the *literary* context which is the Bible (either Jewish or Christian) as a whole and often even the smaller literary context that is the book, the chapter, or whatever. Hans W. Frei points out that when the historical events began to be seen as more indicative of reality than the biblical narratives about them, one casualty was the venerable hermeneutical technique of typology (or figuration).[66] No longer could it be assumed that the various narratives form a coherent sequence, with "earlier and later stories becoming figures one of the other."[67] In truth, the problem extends beyond the question of narrative (which occupies less of the Bible than literary scholars usually think). It soon became impossible to assume that all the texts even belonged to the same religion or theology. To adapt Tertullian, what has Isaiah to do with Qohelet? Or for that matter, the New Testament with the Old? Frei points out that the closest successor to figural reading is the "enterprise called biblical theology, which sought to establish the unity of religious

66. Frei, *Eclipse of Biblical Narrative*, 6.
67. Frei, *Eclipse of Biblical Narrative*, 28.

meaning across the gap of historical and cultural differences."[68] Thus, Walther Eichrodt in the methodological manifesto to his *Theology of the Old Testament* declared that "it is high time that the tyranny of historicism in Old Testament studies was broken." He defined the problem as *"how to understand the realm of Old Testament belief in its structural unity and how, by examining on the one hand its religious environment and on the other its essential coherence with the New Testament, to illuminate its profoundest meaning."*[69] Eichrodt, it appears, wanted to eat his cake and have it too, to reckon with the diachronic perspective that historical consciousness necessitates and to continue to endorse the synchronic perspective that the Christian canon endorses. Unlike a medieval exegete, however, Eichrodt refused to differentiate these methods in terms of distinct senses of Scripture. He thought history would bear out his claim that the Hebrew Bible stands in *"essential coherence"* with the New Testament. It is this notion that accounts for the anti-Judaism that pervades Eichrodt's *Theology,* as when he wrote of "the torso-like appearance of Judaism in separation from Christianity."[70] It is strange that the Jews have never noticed that their tradition is only a torso, especially since Christians have been telling them this for nearly two millennia.

The opposite position to Eichrodt's and that of the Old Testament theologians generally is nicely stated by Boadt, who wrote, you will recall, that "the relationship of the Hebrew Scriptures to the New Testament . . . must begin with the premise that each speaks from its own complete integrity."[71] On

---

68. Frei, *Eclipse of Biblical Narrative,* 8.

69. Eichrodt, *Theology of the Old Testament,* 1:31 (his italics). The first German edition was published in 1933.

70. Eichrodt, *Theology of the Old Testament,* 1:26. See Levenson, "Hebrew Bible in Colleges," 37-40.

71. Boadt, Croner, and Klenicki, *Biblical Studies,* 5.

historicist, or diachronic assumptions, this is, of course, true, but what about the literary, or synchronic perspective? To say that the Hebrew Bible has complete integrity over against the New Testament is to cast grave doubt upon the unity of the Christian Bible. It is like saying one can read the first three acts of *Hamlet* as if the last two did not exist, which is to say that the last two add nothing essential. Now for Christians to say that the New Testament adds nothing essential to the Hebrew Bible is on the order of Marxists' saying that they have no objection to leaving the means of production in the hands of private capitalists. The assertion belies the speakers' announced identity. The supersessionism of an Old Testament theologian like Eichrodt (and he is not atypical) is not adventitious. It is an inevitable corollary of his faith in the unity and integrity of the two-volume Bible of the Church. An unabashedly diachronic approach suggests, as Eichrodt dimly recognized, that the Christian juxtaposition of the Hebrew Bible with the New Testament yields an incoherent book. It is no wonder that some theologians committed to finding meaning in the Scriptures have been retreating from historicism over the past two decades.[72]

One energetic intellectual assault on the historicist approach to the Bible in recent years has come not from theologians, however, but from literary critics, whose methods are more familiar in English departments than in seminaries. Two books in this genre, both published in 1981, present a telling contrast. In *The Great Code*, Northrop Frye offers a modern, secular version of the classic Christian typological reading of the Bible, which for him can only mean the Christian Bible. "I know that

---

72. Most notably Childs, whose "canonical method" relativizes historical criticism without denying its value within the domain of history. See his *Biblical Theology in Crisis; Introduction to the Old Testament;* and *Old Testament Theology.*

Jewish and Islamic conceptions of the Bible are very different," concedes Frye with disarming honesty, "but that is practically all that I do know about them, and it is the Christian Bible that is important for English literature and the Western cultural tradition."[73] In *The Art of Biblical Narrative*, Robert Alter concedes that "there are of course certain literary as well as theological continuities between the Hebrew Bible and the New Testament," but he goes on to say that "the narratives of the latter were written in a different language, at a later time, and, by and large, according to different literary assumptions. It therefore does not seem to me that these two bodies of ancient literature can be comfortably set in the same critical framework."[74] Here I am tempted to invert my remark about Eichrodt and to ask why, if the two testaments do not constitute a profound unity, Christians for thousands of years (including Northrop Frye in our time) have never noticed.

Though neither Frye nor Alter writes as a representative of a religious tradition, and though both seem impatient with theology, the truth is that the unit each chooses for his study is dictated by his heritage, Christianity for Frye, Judaism for Alter. I suppose each could come up with an aesthetic argument for the superiority of his own canon, but the chances of winning over the other would be about as great as the chance that Pablo Christiani or Nachmanides could have won over his opponent in Barcelona in 1263. Whereas historical criticism, with its relativizing and atomizing tendencies, creates a certain neutral ground between Jews and Christians, the new literary criticism, with its concern for typology (or, in Alter's term, "narrative analogy")[75] raises anew the question, Whose Bible? try though

---

73. Frye, *The Great Code*, xiii.
74. Alter, *Art of Biblical Narrative*, ix.
75. Alter, *Art of Biblical Narrative*, 21.

its practitioners do to distance themselves from this old theological hot potato.

A brief and simple example of the difference that context makes should be helpful here. When YHWH, the God of Israel, first makes his covenant with Abraham, the only stipulation is YHWH's self-imposed promise to give Abraham the land, "from the river of Egypt to . . . the river Euphrates" (Gen. 15:17-20).[76] Two chapters later the pact is restated as "an everlasting covenant," symbolized by circumcision (Genesis chapter 17), but again without conditions that the human party must meet for the covenant to endure. Moshe Weinfeld astutely relates this promissory or unconditional covenant to ancient Near Eastern grants, in which the greater king rewards the lesser for "loyalty and good deeds already performed." This "covenant of grant" he distinguishes from the more familiar "treaty," in which the suzerain offers his vassal "an inducement for future loyalty" and the keynote is one of stern conditionality.[77] Whether the next covenant of which we read, that of Sinai in the generation of Moses, was originally conceived along the lines of a treaty is hard to determine; certainly, most of the Torah does indeed so conceive it now. The dichotomy of treaty and grant, however, can obscure the important point that the Patriarchal grant is not parallel with the Mosaic treaty, but, instead, intersects with it on Sinai. In the incident of the golden calf, Israel violates the conditions of covenant just concluded and brings about a divine threat of annihilation (Exod. 32:9-10). It is precisely the Patriarchal grant that Moses invokes to avert the evil decree:

76. All biblical quotes here are taken from *Tanakh*.
77. Weinfeld, "Covenant of Grant," 85. See also Levenson, *Sinai and Zion*, 97-101. The terminology here is misleading, in that Weinfeld's "grant" would itself appear to be a species of treaty, that is, a treaty with an unconditional component.

> Remember Your servants, Abraham, Isaac, and Jacob, how You swore to them by Your Self and said to them: I will make your offspring as numerous as the stars of heaven, and I will give to your offspring this whole land of which I spoke, to possess forever (Exod. 32:13; cf. Deut. 9:27).

Nothing is more typical of the treaty as opposed to the grant than long lists of blessings and curses, yet after the list in Leviticus, we again hear of the Patriarchal Covenant, that is, the grant. When, heartsick in exile, having grievously desecrated the stipulations of Sinai, Israel shall confess their iniquity and humble their proud heart, "then will I remember My covenant with Jacob; I will remember My covenant with Isaac, and also My covenant with Abraham; and I will remember the land" (Lev. 26:39-42).

The result of the intersection on Sinai of these two types of covenants, the grant and the treaty, is a type of spiritual relationship between the people Israel and their God that is not reducible to either component. The perpetual land grant to the Patriarchs has come to serve as a platform upon which the shaky structure of the Mosaic Covenant can rest securely. Human fallibility, the lethal threat to any conditional relationship, is countered by a prior and irrevocable divine oath to the ancestors of the errant community. Both Israel's unqualified obligation to observe the מצוות and God's indefeasible promise to Abraham remain in force. This interlacing of covenants is characteristic not only of the Hebrew Bible, but of rabbinic Judaism as well, where the grant to Abraham is transformed into the idea of the "merit of the Fathers" (זכות אבות) that Israel's transgressions can never altogether nullify.

Such is the picture if we limit the unit to be interpreted to the Hebrew Bible. You will recall, however, that I have argued that though a certain sense of Scripture requires this limitation,

Christians must ultimately aim for another sense as well, one that upholds the idea that their two-volume Bible is a meaningful whole. If we include the New Testament in our interpretation of Abraham, we must reckon with Paul's belief that God's pre-Sinaitic commitment to Abraham shows the possibility of justification apart from the Torah, at least for gentiles (Galatians chapter 3; Romans chapter 4). Instead of Abraham's serving as a kind of platform upon which Torah and commandments (מצוות) can stand firmly despite the innate human impulse to evil, he serves Paul as a kind of circumferential highway that enables one to bypass Sinai altogether and still reach God, as one never could, in fact, through Sinai itself. On this reading, the emphasis shifts from the integration of grant and treaty on Sinai to their original separation.[78] Abraham no longer prefigures the hope of a contrite Israel in exile, but rather the justification of the Christian apart from the works of the Law and even from the people Israel. Of course, this extreme position of Paul's would have to be qualified by consideration of other New Testament documents, especially James, for the author of which Abraham was justified by faith and deeds conjointly (James 2:14-26). The fact remains, however, that just as each piece on a chessboard changes the meaning and value of every other piece, so does each text in the Bible change our reading of all the others. The first three acts of *Hamlet* will never be the same after the last two have been read.[79]

---

78. One can find the Pauline interpretation in von Rad, "Faith Reckoned as Righteousness." Von Rad's conclusion—that "only faith . . . brings man into a right relationship with God"—implies an exclusion that is not to be found in his text (Gen. 15:6) or, for that matter, anywhere else in the Hebrew Bible. His commitment to Paul's Abraham was so intense that he overlooked altogether its contradiction with the Torah's Abraham, his ostensible subject. See Levenson, "Why Jews Are Not Interested," 300-304.

79. See Levenson, "Eighth Principle of Judaism," 218-25.

We can always choose, of course, to limit our investigation to a smaller corpus, for example, to any one of the passages just mentioned. This is what פשטנות, the medieval Jewish pursuit of the historico-grammatical, or literal sense, did. On this narrowest context, Jews and Christians can work together, just as they can on modern historical investigation. Indeed, these types of study are done best by those scholars who can bracket their religious commitments or have none to bracket, as the whole sorry history of religious bias in biblical studies amply demonstrates. In the realm of historical criticism, pleas for a "Jewish biblical scholarship" or a "Christian biblical scholarship" are senseless and reactionary. Practicing Jews and Christians will differ from uncompromising historicists, however, in affirming the meaningfulness and interpretive relevance of larger contexts that homogenize the literatures of different periods to one degree or another. Just as text has more than one context, and biblical studies more than one method, so Scripture has more than one sense, as the medievals knew and Tyndale, Spinoza, Jowett, and most other moderns have forgotten. As the context gets larger, Jews and Christians can still work together, as each empathizes imaginatively with the other's distinctive context. But empathy is not identity, and if the Bible (under whatever definition) is to be seen as having coherence and theological integrity, there will come a moment in which Jewish-Christian consensus becomes existentially impossible.

CONCLUSION

Historical criticism has indeed brought about a new situation in biblical studies. The principal novelty lies in the recovery of the Hebrew Bible as opposed to the *Tanakh* and the Old Testament affirmed by rabbinic Judaism and Christianity, respectively. Jews and Christians can indeed meet as equals in the study of this new/old book, but only because the Hebrew Bible is largely foreign to both traditions and precedes them. This meeting of Jews and Christians on neutral ground can have great value, for it helps to correct misconceptions each group has of the other and to prevent the grievous consequences of such misconceptions, such as anti-Semitic persecutions. It is also the case that some of the insights into the text that historical criticism generates will be appropriated by the Jews or the Church themselves, who can thereby convert history into tradition and add vitality to an exegetical practice become stale and repetitive. But it is also the case that the historical-critical method compels its practitioners to bracket their traditional identities, and this renders its ability to enrich Judaism and Christianity problematic. There is, to be sure, plenty of room in each tradition for such bracketing. There are ample precedents for Jews to pursue a plain sense at odds with rabbinic Midrashim and even *halakhah* and for Christians to interpret the Old Testament in a nonchristocentic fashion. But unless historical criticism can learn to interact with other senses of Scripture—senses peculiar to the individual traditions and not shared between them—it will either fade or prove to be not a meeting ground of Jews and Christians, but the burial ground of Judaism and Christianity, as each tradition vanishes into the past in which neither had as yet emerged. Western Christians are so used to being in the majority that the danger of vanishing is usually not real to them; after all, the post-Christian era will still be post-Christian, not post-something else. But Jewry, none too numerous before the Holocaust, has now become "a brand plucked from the fire" (Zech. 3:2), and most Jews with an active commitment to their tradition will be suspicious of any allegedly common ground that requires them to suppress or shed their Jewishness. Bracketing tradition has its value, but also its limitations. Though fundamentalists will not see the value, nor historicists the limitations, intellectual integrity and spiritual vitality in this new situation demand the careful affirmation of both.

Theological Honesty through History

JOSEPH BLENKINSOPP

Jon D. Levenson raises a serious issue about the current uncontentious involvement of Jews and Christians in the academic study of the Bible. The same issue, one recalls, was raised by Moshe Goshen-Gottstein in 1975,[1] when he spoke of the post-World War II "objectivity syndrome" and of escape into specialization. Levenson suspects that this situation has come about as a result of the suspension or perhaps absence of confessional commitments and a tacit agreement not to pursue such theological implications as would inevitably highlight the profound differences between Judaism and Christianity. As the title of his paper suggests, he believes that the historical-critical method, which has dominated the study of biblical texts since the Enlightenment, provides the cover necessary for this evasion to be maintained. He warns that this situation of benign coexistence is no substitute for serious discussion of the theological claims arising out of the respective canons of Christian and Jew.

While I suspect that Levenson is not far off the mark with respect to the confessional stance of Christian biblical scholars,

---

1. See Goshen-Gottstein, "Christianity, Judaism, and Modern Bible Study," 69-88.

appearances can be deceptive. The main problem, at any rate, seems to be rather the disjunction between the study of the Bible in the academy and its use in the churches. There seem to be several factors at work here. With the exception of those institutions of higher learning which have maintained an explicitly confessional orientation, the university tends to impose a kind of discourse quite different from that of the seminary, church, or synagogue, and its predominantly secular atmosphere is not one in which interreligious dialogue or polemic breathes freely. Biblical scholars, both Christian and Jewish but especially Christian, are also constantly being reminded of the intense pressure exerted by fundamentalist biblicism which is neither critical nor historical.

Perhaps the most important reason for reticence (rather than evasion) on the part of the Christian biblical scholar is, however, the awareness that the confessional positions adopted heretofore, which have come to expression in numerous theologies of the Old and New Testament, have been almost invariably such as to preclude Jewish participation in advance. Levenson's allusion to the work of Martin Noth and Walther Eichrodt, both still very influential, will serve as a reminder of the persistence of such schemata based on very explicit confessional premises. We must move on, of course, but no one aware of this situation will be tempted to underestimate either the dead weight of the past or the positive aspects of the current theological neutrality.

Levenson rightly draws our attention to the normative claims implicit in the different ways of dividing up biblical history. Those familiar with nineteenth- and early twentieth-century theologies of the Old Testament will recall that tripartite divisions—e.g. *Mosaismus, Prophetismus, Judaismus*—were practically de rigueur, and will have no difficulty recognizing the thesis of historical degeneration underlying such arrangements.

At this point we come up against the problem of the canon or canons much discussed in recent years. It is well known that the term itself is of Christian vintage, being first used with reference to the biblical books by Athanasius around the middle of the fourth century (in his *Decrees of the Synod of Nicaea* around 350 rather than, as is often stated, in the *Festal Letter* of 367). Jews and Christians acknowledge a biblical canon, of course, but for both canonicity is functionally different. In Judaism, functional canonicity includes Mishnah and Talmud, the relation of which to the Bible is sometimes explicit but more often difficult to detect. In Catholic Christianity, tradition—understood with reference to a theory of the development of doctrine—is functionally on the same level as Scripture, though at times eventuating in positions whose relation to the biblical data is not easily perceived. The Anglican communion, to take one more example, has traditionally accorded special status to developments within the first four Christian centuries. Reflection on this "canon outside of the canon" will, I suggest, prove more productive than an undue emphasis accorded to the "canon within the canon" (rightly criticized by Rolf Rendtorff in this volume).

Acknowledgment of functional canonicity would, at the least, make it easier for us to see unbroken lines of development originating in a corpus of writings held in common (*Tanakh*, the Old Testament), lines which lead to the classical formulation of the two faiths following quite different hermeneutical principles. This basic Scripture would then more clearly emerge as the common basis and starting point for distinct religious traditions, each with its own identity and integrity, traditions which are mutually interactive and the study of which could be mutually illuminating.

In view of this situation we can appreciate the problem posed by the Reformers' allegiance to the principle of *sola scriptura*, especially since the *scriptura* in question was identified with the Massoretic Bible. In his *Holy Scripture: Canon, Authority, Criticism*, James Barr commented on the dilemma arising out of a doctrinal formulation (*sola scriptura*) purportedly founded on biblical warranty and therefore on a scriptural canon not itself guaranteed by biblical warranty.[2] One result was to emphasize the discontinuity between Second Temple Judaism, or at least the postbiblical part of it, and early Christianity. As Julius Wellhausen put it more than a century ago (on the first page of his *Prolegomena*), "Judaism is a mere empty chasm over which one springs from the Old Testament to the New." Early Judaism, in other words, was something quite different from the religion of Israel on the one side and from early Christianity on the other.

It must also seem unfortunate, in retrospect, that inner-Christian polemic dictated canonical closure in the subapostolic period, with the result that only those writings were included which reflect, in different ways and with different emphases, the painful separation of the Christian movement from the parent body. The tendency to idealize group origins, which seems to go with the idea of canonicity, would therefore have to be balanced by a sober historical appreciation of the circumstances under which the New Testament writings came into existence.

One can only agree with Levenson's criticism of a historicist approach that neglects literary contexts, that is unaccompanied by a "hermeneutic of retrieval," and that easily degenerates into a "trivializing antiquarianism." Even if we remain less than totally convinced by some of the alternatives now offered

---

2. Barr, *Holy Scripture*, 23.

(including structuralism, deconstructionism, canonical criticism), we will readily agree that the historical-critical method has often gone in tandem with historical relativism or served the purposes of confessional ideology. The obvious example of the latter is the Documentary Hypothesis, now in the process of disintegration, which was almost from the beginning in the service of a theory of religious (that is, Jewish) degeneration.

I am convinced, notwithstanding, that it would be a serious error to abandon the historical-critical reading of biblical texts. There are levels of meaning in biblical texts, and channels of communication between text and reader, accessible only through this kind of inquiry. Contrary to Brevard Childs's contention, the final form of the text is not the only appropriate object of theological reflection.[3] If, for example, it can be critically ascertained that the message of Amos himself was quite different from that of the book in its final form—as most would admit is the case—this would be an important datum not just historically but theologically. History works to keep theology honest, and we are always faced with the challenge of critically reconstructing and reappropriating the past if we are to know what direction to take into the future.

The conclusion I would draw from Levenson's paper is not that we should set about writing a different kind of Old Testament theology—we are nowhere close to knowing how to do that as yet—but that Jewish and Christian scholars should collaborate in the theological interpretation of texts of the Scripture which they hold in common. Those who have read Levenson's admirable *Creation and the Persistence of Evil*,[4] will appreciate how much the Christian may learn from a

3. See Childs, *Introduction to the Old Testament*, xx.
4. Levenson, *Creation and the Persistence of Evil*.

distinctively Jewish treatment of a central biblical theme. Speaking again from the Christian perspective, there will be the challenge to familiarize oneself with alternative exegetical traditions, to enter into the inner logic of the Midrash, to recover some of the insights of the great medieval *darshanim* for ourselves and our students. And, as noted more than once in this volume, one corollary might well be that the Christian interpreter will be led to extend his or her knowledge of Hebrew beyond the relatively narrow band of the biblical dialect. All of this may not be quite what Levenson is looking for, but it should at least bring us beyond the point of historicist evasion if not quite to the point of theological consensus.

Different Texts or Different Quests?
The Contexts of Biblical Studies

DAVID LEVENSON

The central question addressed in this book—To what extent are Jewish and Christian scholars working on the Hebrew Bible or Old Testament engaged in a common enterprise?—has led, not surprisingly, to a number of other, related questions:

- Does the quest for the "original" meaning of a biblical text establish a common ground?
- What is the value of historical-critical scholarship for the study of the meaning of the biblical text? How does it compare to the traditional interpretations produced by the Jewish and Christian communities?
- How do different conceptions of text and canon affect our considerations of these questions?
- Can Jews and Christians produce a common biblical theology?

A helpful way of approaching these questions is to consider separately the two different institutional contexts in which many biblical scholars do their work: the professional guild devoted to the academic study of the history and literature of the ancient Israelite community, and their own Jewish or Christian religious community.

THE OPEN ACADEMY

Biblical scholars identifying themselves as Jews or Christians belong to the same faculties and professional organizations, read and write papers for one another, teach courses with similar content, and generally believe they are engaged in a common enterprise. What they seem to share is a commitment to what has traditionally been called historical criticism (more precisely designated historical-literary criticism). Practitioners of this approach share an interest in such issues as reconstructing the circumstances that gave rise to the text, understanding its meanings in a variety of literary and historical contexts (from the perspective of both author and reader or listener), and tracing the history of ideas it contains. If we define historical-literary criticism institutionally, that is, the content and methods characteristic of members of a professional organization like the Society of Biblical Literature, then it includes today a wide variety of literary and social-scientific methods, both synchronic and diachronic. It takes into account the multiplicity of meanings in a text at each moment of its various stages of development. Historical-literary criticism no longer focuses exclusively on the one original meaning of a text or is concerned solely with such questions as the forms of Psalms, the sources of Genesis, and the historicity of the conquest narrative.

An important feature of the study of the Bible in this institutional context is that it is not limited to members of particular religious communities. The only commitment required is to a principle generally accepted in the academy: the methods of analysis employed and the evidence adduced must be accessible to everyone. In fact, if Jews and Christians were to disappear, there would be no reason for the *Journal of Biblical Literature* to stop publication. The analysis of the religion, history, and literature of ancient Israel would still be an important subject of enquiry. In the setting of the open academy, there is a great deal of truth in Jon D. Levenson's observation that to the extent that Jews and Christians pursue a common agenda, they do it neither as Jews nor as Christians.[1]

Of course, many who pursue historical-literary criticism in the open academy are, at the same time, believing Jews and Christians, with a commitment to their own religious communities. Their reconstructions and analyses of the world of ancient Israel are often deeply influenced by theological concerns. Levenson and James L. Kugel have demonstrated how a Protestant bias has shaped the agenda of historical criticism in the past century.

Few of us would dispute the fact that, for many scholars, theological interests have determined the choice of particular texts for study, the questions asked, the methods used, and the results obtained. But religious affiliation and outlook are not the only factors that can influence a scholar's work. Where, when, and with whom one studied are usually at least as influential as theological outlook, and there are a host of other psychological and sociological factors at work that are much less susceptible to self-criticism because they are much harder for us to discern.

Although it would be naive to play down the influence of conscious or unconscious biases, they do, I believe, have a greater impact on certain kinds of questions. Jews and Christians might well find their backgrounds intruding less in discussions of more or less objective questions, those that could be easily resolved if we had a time machine: What was the

---

1. See Jon D. Levenson's essay in this volume, "Theological Consensus or Historicist Evasion? Jews and Christians in Biblical Studies."

exemplar of a particular manuscript? Where was a particular site located? When, by whom, and using what sources was a text written? But when we turn to the history of ideas, such as a descriptive account of biblical theology (which I would prefer to call the study of the religious ideas of ancient Israel), the perspective and particular interests of the interpreter play a greater role. The selection of evidence from a text, the choice of comparative material from outside the text, the formation of categories, and the tracing of lines of development are all highly subjective activities.

The best way to deal with the inevitable fact of our biases is to make sure that as many voices as possible are heard. The greater the diversity of backgrounds of those engaged in any humanistic enterprise, the richer and broader the questions asked and the less likely it is that one ideological perspective will masquerade as the objective one.

In some cases, a particular ideological perspective might lead to a better appreciation of an ancient phenomenon, as, for instance, feminist scholarship has revolutionized the history of early Christianity. A sympathetic presentation of the Northern Kingdom might well reflect a Protestant bias, as Kugel and Levenson argue;[2] but that, it seems to me, enhances, rather than limits, our historical imagination. A problem emerges when only one perspective is represented, one historical reconstruction dogmatically affirmed, or one original meaning sought.

For those engaged in historical-literary criticism, the question of canon is important on a number of levels. The development of the idea of the canon inside and outside of Scripture is an important sociohistorical question, and the

2. See Jon D. Levenson's essay in this volume ("Theological Consensus?"), citing Kugel, "Biblical Studies," 22, and extending his argument.

difference it makes in understanding the context in which a particular text is read is an important literary question.

Outside of religious communities, however, the canon of a particular group should not dictate the temporal, or, for that matter, any other boundaries within which a phenomenon is investigated. Of course, practical considerations impose a limit on how much any one individual can study. In practice, religious interests, both of the scholar and of the audience for his or her teaching and writing, often play a role in defining boundaries of research. Nevertheless, these decisions, like the one to limit the study of the Hebrew Bible to the period in which the text was first produced (or to ancient Jewish interpretations that might serve as background for the New Testament) do not follow inevitably from historical-literary criticism.

If we understand canon as the list of documents that define and shape a community's identity, we should also consider the canon of historical-literary critics: those primary and secondary texts that keep appearing on graduate student reading lists and that tend to define our questions, methods, and subjects. We deceive ourselves dangerously if we think we can avoid such a canon. We must, however, make sure it is constantly open to revision and reflects a variety of perspectives. No doubt the canonical status of such works as Gerhard von Rad's and Walther Eichrodt's theologies of the Old Testament plays a large part in the Jewish suspicion of German Protestant biblical criticism in general and of biblical theology in particular.[3]

A question related to the professional canon is the study of the history of exegesis within the context of historical-literary criticism. No doubt many believe that a christological reading of the Old Testament and a rabbinic reading of the Hebrew Bible

3. See Jon D. Levenson's essay in this volume ("Theological Consensus?"); see also, Levenson, "Why Jews Are Not Interested," 281-307.

represent the baggage that historical-literary criticism has worked hard to shed, and that such interpretations would immediately sabotage the reading of the text in any sort of pluralistic context. On the other hand, now that the belief in a single historical meaning of the text is beginning to be questioned on literary and theoretical grounds, there is an increasing sense that ignoring the various traditional interpretations might rob us of an invaluable resource for imagining what the text meant, has meant, and could mean.[4]

I take the growing interest in the history of exegesis among biblical scholars in the academy to reflect a renewed interest in the multiplicity of meanings present in any literary text. There is also a recognition that the study of a text need not be limited to the period in which it was first produced and that there is a dialectical relationship between the meaning of a text and the community that produces that meaning. Problems arise only when traditional interpretations are given a greater authority than other interpretations, or when they are used anachronistically. We can agree that Isaiah could not have been referring to Jesus or that the Midrash does not offer us independent evidence of the Patriarchal period. Both Christian and Jewish interpretations of Scripture, however, are now being taken into account by scholars—Jewish, Christian, or those who are neither—wanting to explore not only the phenomena of postbiblical Judaism and Christianity, but also the phenomenon of meaning in texts.

Levenson argues that those engaged in historical criticism might have thrown out the baby with the bathwater in their attempt to limit their work to neutral ground from which religious commitments are banished.[5] It is true that scholarship

4. See James L. Kugel's essay in this volume, "Cain and Abel in Fact and Fable: Genesis 4:1-16."

5. See Jon D. Levenson's essay in this volume ("Theological Consensus?")

primarily addressing the concerns of a particular religious community, at least in theory, has no place in the institutional context I have been describing. This does not mean, however, that historical-literary criticism as practiced in the open academy must be regarded as devoid of larger values. The values it instills are the values of any humanistic historical or literary study. While these are not necessarily the values of the text itself, they are precisely those values that can be shared by all scholars regardless of religious commitment or lack thereof. Grappling with the meaning of a text, studying how our past and the past of others is reconstructed and represented to us, and developing in ourselves and teaching others an empathy for those living in different times and places all serve to enlarge our sensibility about the human condition. When these tasks are applied to a text that has had a unique influence on Western culture and ideology, I see little danger that such study will degenerate into irrelevant antiquarianism or become the sole preserve of those interested only in debunking traditional values.

THE RELIGIOUS COMMUNITY

Are Jewish and Christian Biblical scholars engaged in a common enterprise when they work within their respective communities? To a limited extent they are, since most communities have a clear interest in the results of historical-literary criticism. When they describe what the text meant, how it has been interpreted, and even, as James A. Sanders reminds us, which text is read,[6] historical-literary critics can provide important resources for church and synagogue. By displaying the tradition in its full historical variety, they offer the

---

6. See James A. Sanders's essay in this volume, "Hebrew Bible *and* Old Testament: Textual Criticism in Service of Biblical Studies."

community more options from which to create new meanings, and by reminding the community that traditional interpretations cannot naively be identified with the text's original meaning, they undercut claims of religious exclusiveness.

It is when Jewish and Christian biblical scholars relate their work to the needs of their own religious groups that they must part company. The task of giving contemporary meaning to Scripture is an act of communal self-definition. The recovery of the various meanings of the biblical text in the periods in which it took shape and throughout the history of its interpretation might be of interest to most Jewish and Christian communities, but how this information is used in the hermeneutical process varies considerably from community to community.

For Protestant communities, the question of the original meanings is a more pressing issue than for Jews and Catholics, who have other means of self-definition. It is no accident that Protestants have been the leaders in historical criticism and therefore have set much of its agenda. It is also not unusual for Protestant biblical scholars to double as theologians, because their findings will in many communities have normative status.

Increasing contacts with Jews and Catholics, a growing cultural respect for tradition and, no doubt, many other factors as well, appear to have led to a greater appreciation of the history of exegesis in Protestant circles. There still seems to be a tendency, however, for many Protestants to regard traditional interpretations, to the extent that they do not directly illuminate the original meanings of the text, as edifying, but not in any sense normative for what the text means within the community. The history of Jewish exegesis often becomes most important not for the light it sheds on the religious life of ancient Israel, including the Old Testament, but for the extent to which it illuminates the background of the New Testament.

The relationship between Scripture and tradition in Roman Catholicism and the appropriation of and attitude toward the historical-critical method are exceedingly complex questions. Suffice it to say that the past quarter of a century has seen an explosion in Roman Catholic biblical scholarship, most of it done within Catholic institutions. What is astonishing, at least to an outsider, is not only the quantity and quality of this work, but also the number of superb popular surveys making the results of modern biblical scholarship accessible to those outside the guild. It is, no doubt, too early to tell what the long-term impact of this will be on faith and practice, but certainly Catholic theology can never be only biblical theology. In competition with American Protestantism, Roman Catholicism will have to continue to stress the importance of tradition as a means of establishing self-identity. Perhaps what appears to be a renewed interest in the history of exegesis reflects this competition, as well as the other general cultural factors that have generated interest in traditional interpretation among Protestants and Jews. Here it is of interest to note that Catholics have less reason to end their interest in Jewish exegesis in the first century than have Protestants, both because of the importance of Jewish interpretation for the ancient and medieval church and perhaps also because of a greater interest in nonliteral modes of scriptural interpretation.

The Reform, Conservative, and Reconstructionist Jewish seminaries all teach historical-literary criticism. This is not surprising, since one of the chief ways the movements they represent distinguish themselves from Orthodoxy is their emphasis on the process of the historical development of the Jewish people and its ideas and culture. This reflects not only a post-Enlightenment rejection of biblical inerrancy, but also th fascination of most modern Jews with history. It is, after all, a common history rather than theology (or even law) that offers the primary means of self-definition for the great majority of Jews today.

Having said this, it must be recognized that for all modern Jews, rabbinic exegesis of Scripture is normative in the sense that it provides a touchstone for what makes an interpretation of a text Jewish. Midrash is recognized as a Jewish art form, the primary means of transmitting moral edification, and one of the authoritative means of establishing *halakhic* practice. Reform, Conservative, and Reconstructionist Jews would not hesitate to accept the findings of historical criticism that "an eye for an eye" might have originally been understood literally, but they would each see it as a great advance of the rabbis to interpret the *lex talionis* in terms of monetary compensation. Similarly, it is irrelevant for Jewish practice whether "You shall not boil a kid in its mother's milk" might have originally meant something other than the commandment not to eat meat and milk together. It is the rabbinic tradition which is normative for all Jews who keep kosher.

And, of course, the tradition is not only important as a source of *halakhah*. Few Jews would want to promote a Jewish reading of the Bible that deprived them of the aesthetic pleasure or moral insight of Midrash Aggadah. Even the most radical Classical Reformers, who rejected much of rabbinic law and lore on the grounds that it was postbiblical and who made historical criticism one of the cornerstones of the movement, w themselves as heirs of the Pharisees who were willing to pt outmoded biblical concepts to new ideas. It is hard to ine a Jewish theology that would grant greater authority to ʒinal meaning of the text than to rabbinic interpretation.

superficial sketch of the different functions of literary criticism of the Bible and the study of traditional interpretations in the context of particular religious communities should not be taken to mean that Jews have nothing to learn from Christian readings of the Old Testament and that Christians have nothing to learn from Jewish readings of the Hebrew Bible. In the context of the open academy, Jews and Christians can read each other's work, along with that of non-Jews and non-Christians, to keep their own work balanced. In the context of the religious community, each side should read the other's interpretation to appreciate what they have in common and possibly to adopt and adapt insights that might enrich their own tradition. Even more important, however, it will help them understand and learn to respect the differences between them. This might lead to greater sensitivity to the faith of the other, for many an important religious value in and of itself. As Sanders puts it, when we interpret our own Scriptures, we should imagine members of other communities listening.[7] I might add that this suggestion should be institutionalized by providing a Christian presence in every Jewish seminary and a Jewish presence in every Christian seminary or theological faculty.

Rolf Rendtorff has made a forceful and compassionate plea for a common Jewish-Christian reading of the Bible, focusing on theological ideas.[8] The question is not, to my mind, so much whether this is a good idea, as much as in what institutional context this should take place. As I have indicated, I think it is imperative for biblical scholars from each tradition to hear the voice of the other as they address the academy and the church or synagogue. If the goal of a common reading is to promote sensitivity toward the other, this should be done within the

---

7. See James A. Sanders's essay in this volume ("Hebrew Bible *and* Old Testament").

8. See Rolf Rendtorff's essay in this volume, "Toward a Common Jewish-Christian Reading of the Hebrew Bible."

respective communities. If it is to produce a common description of the religious ideas of ancient Israel that is relatively free from religious bias, it should be done in the academy. But if the goal is to create a new common theology for the individual communities that is based on the original or historical meanings of the Hebrew Scriptures, I doubt there will be many takers.

Part Three

Reading Religious Texts
in Community

Cain and Abel in Fact and Fable: Genesis 4:1-16

JAMES L. KUGEL

I should like in the following essay to examine a particular biblical text and its history, and so seek to provide a somewhat different perspective on the more general issue of Jewish and Christian approaches to biblical interpretation. The text in question is the brief account of Cain and Abel in chapter 4 of Genesis. That chapter, it will be recalled, recounts how the brothers Cain and Abel, a farmer and a shepherd, resolve to offer up sacrifices to God. Cain's sacrifice, in keeping with his profession, comes from the "fruit of the ground," while Abel's comes from his flocks; Abel's sacrifice is apparently preferred by God, and this turn of events so angers Cain that he eventually kills his brother and, when his crime is discovered, is sentenced by God to a life of eternal wandering. Such is the bare outline of the Genesis account.

This text, as will be seen shortly, presents a number of difficulties to the exegete and has inspired all manner of explanations and elaborations throughout the history of biblical interpretation. But before turning to the history of its exegesis, I should like to consider briefly the story itself in order to ask the sort of questions about it that a modern biblical scholar might pose: What is it *really* about? Why was it written? And how can one explain some of the puzzling details of the narrative as well as several mysterious features of its language? A thorough consideration of these questions might foreclose treatment of any others, so let me content myself here with a rapid description of the current scholarly consensus, to the extent that one exists.[1]

BIBLICAL HISTORIOGRAPHY

The story of Cain and Abel, like so many early biblical narratives, seems actually to be concerned with explaining events or everyday reality of a period long after the time when the story itself is set. This is the broadly etiological side of biblical historiography: the past is presented as having determined the course of later history. So, for example, the account of Jacob's struggles with his brother Esau was apparently put forward in biblical times as a way of explaining the political relations of the descendents of these two figures, respectively the peoples of Israel and of Edom: Why are Israel and Edom—though so similar in language, culture, and no doubt blood—constantly at each other's throats? It all goes back to their ancestors and founders, Jacob and Esau: these two were brothers, indeed, twins (an expression of similarity and kinship), but they never could get along, in fact they even fought in utero. Hence, primordial events explain later reality. And in regard to the same theme of relations between Israel and Esau/Edom, how is it that a once-small tribal entity came for a time to dominate its originally larger neighbor? This too is foretold in the doings of their ancestors, in the oracle given to

1. A substantial secondary literature exists on the subject of Cain and Abel and, in particualar, the Kenites (see below). Some of the major works in this bibliography are cited in Kalimi's recent article, "Three Assumptions about the Kenites," 386-93.

Rebecca before Jacob and Esau were even born, in the sale of Esau's birthright to Jacob, and in Jacob's obtaining by trickery a paternal blessing originally intended for his brother. Family events of the past explain tribal reality of the present.

Similarly, a modern scholar might say, the story of Cain and Abel is really a story aimed at explaining Cain's descendants (Abel, thanks to his being murdered, had none)—that wild, nomadic tribe known as the Kenites, whose traces appear elsewhere in biblical narrative. How is it, an ancient Israelite might have asked, that these Kenites are so ferocious, inflicting (according to the biblical evidence itself)[2] retribution on their enemies far out of keeping with established practice? And by what right? From the standpoint of a modern scholar, the tale of Cain seems to have been designed to answer just such questions, and, more specifically, to provide the same sort of historical explanation of then-current reality that the narratives of Jacob and Esau and other biblical stories provided. The Kenites are murderous, this story seeks to explain, because they are all descended from an original murderer—for in biblical genetics it is axiomatic that the founder's chromosomes are passed on with unvarying accuracy from generation to generation. As for the Kenites' *right* to be murderous, is it not contained in the punchline of our story, "Anyone who kills Cain will suffer vengeance sevenfold" (Gen. 4:15)? This sentence, uttered by God to Cain, amounts to a divine exception to the *lex talionis*: the Kenite practice of killing seven of yours to avenge one of theirs is "grandfathered" (as it were) to them in the story of their ancestor Cain, who, protesting the eternal wandering which the Deity decrees for him as punishment for murdering Abel, is then granted by God this right of taking

2. This is implied in both Gen. 4:15 and Gen. 4:24.

exceptional vengeance, seven for one instead of one for one, as a means of warding off would-be marauders.

Indeed, the etiological character of our story is made clearest in that very verse. For if the story were really only about an individual named Cain, rather than about that individual as representative of a tribe called the Kenites, then the Hebrew of Gen. 4:15 would probably be slightly different: it would not say, as it does, כל הרג קין, "Any who kill Cain" (for this in biblical Hebrew implies a whole group, a class of murderers—and why should a whole class of murderers be bent on killing a single individual, Cain?), but ההורג קין or even האיש אשר יהרוג את קין— i.e. "Cain's killer," "the one who kills Cain." The potential plurality of killers envisaged in the phrase כל הרג קין seems to indicate that "Cain" in this sentence really means "a Kenite" (just as, incidentally, elsewhere in the Bible "Aaron" regularly means "an Aaronide," "David" can mean a "Davidide," and so forth). Indeed, this phrase ought to be compared to כל מכה יבוסי ("Anyone who kills a Jebusite") in 2 Sam. 5:8, where the plurality of envisaged killers and victims is indisputable. And so our text is really a way of leading up to, and offering a plausible justification for, that significant sentence, "Anyone who kills a Kenite will suffer sevenfold vengeance." It was pronounced by God as a compensation for Cain's punishment—nomads like him need not be limited to the relative civility of one-for-one vengeance.

Now of course this is not all that modern scholarship might put forward in approaching our narrative. There is, for example, the (admittedly now somewhat threadbare) "Kenite hypothesis" of the late nineteenth and early twentieth centuries, according to which the Kenites were a nomadic tribe that—strangely—seems to have worshipped the same Deity as Israel. Indeed, it was the Kenites (according to this theory) who had originally introduced Israel to the worship of this Deity, such introduction being represented in our Bible by the close contact between Moses and Jethro, the Midianite/Kenite priest, just before the Sinai Revelation.[3] This Kenite hypothesis has some attractive features to it—I have not stated them here—but it also suffered from a basic shortage of evidence, and has not fared well in recent evaluations. This notwithstanding, a subscriber to the notion that the Kenites did worship the same Deity as the Israelites might see in our story of Cain and Abel an attempt to account for this circumstance as well, which would surely have struck later Israelites as somewhat bizarre. And so our story relates that Cain, the tribal ancestor of the Kenites, was not always a wanderer, and did not always dwell outside of the land in which the God of Israel holds particular sway. He once dwelled on our land, but was expelled for the crime of murder. This circumstance explains the fact that his descendents continue to worship our God, and, as well, explains their own murderous character and apparent unwillingness to abide by the principle of equal retribution that our God apparently endorses within his territory.

There are other matters to which we might turn: nothing has been said, for example, of the somewhat mysterious "sign" that God grants to Cain to help ward off danger during his wanderings. But I trust that the foregoing portrays accurately at least some of the sorts of concerns that modern scholars might bring to an understanding of the overall shape and purpose of this biblical text. Methodologically, the foregoing is indebted in no small measure to the work of the late-nineteenth- and twentieth-century German scholar Hermann Gunkel, whose "Form Critical" approach to biblical writings has exercised broad influence on scholars throughout the world. Other biblical texts

---

3. Stade, working on the suggestions of earlier scholars, set out this theory in his *Geschichte des Volkes Israel*, 1:126; it was subsequently taken up by Budde and other writers.

might have brought us to consider more the question of narrative sources underlying the final form of a particular story (or "Source Criticism," as this approach is generally known). Yet other critical questions might have turned out attention to the area of textual comparison between the traditional Hebrew version of our Bible and other ancient textual witnesses: the Old Greek Bible (whose underlying Hebrew original was somewhat different from our traditional Hebrew text), the Samaritan Pentateuch, and so forth.

These methods and concerns of modern biblical scholarship may serve to highlight the enormous gap between ourselves and the approaches adopted by ancient biblical scholars, Jews and Christians, to the same questions. I daresay these ancient scholars were no less serious about the task of biblical exegesis; nor were they, in some respects, any less sophisticated. But what a difference there is in the sorts of questions that they sought to ask of the Bible, and in the methods that they used in trying to find answers! To begin with, ancient exegetes, whether Jews or Christians, were not interested in understanding biblical stories from the standpoint of Israelites who may have lived a thousand years earlier: they were interested in what the text had to say to their own times, and—here is the point—they were by and large convinced that the Bible could be, and ought to be, read in just such terms. This was because, for them, the Bible was first and foremost a book of divine instruction. It was the God-given manual of life, and in scrutinizing its pages one could find (though, admittedly, often only by resorting to the cleverest or most penetrating sorts of analysis, for divine truth was regularly presented in the Bible in hidden form) messages concerning the weightiest issues in human existence: how one ought to live one's life on earth; what it is that God desires that we do; what the future holds for humankind. And so biblical stories and songs and the like were not explained in terms of the environment and historical setting in which they were first transmitted, but were read as messages of current validity, containing teachings about right conduct and the Divine Plan.

A TALE OF GOOD AND EVIL

We shall eventually turn to the question of how this particular attitude toward the Bible developed in early exegesis, but for now, let us illustrate it with some concrete examples in connection with the story of Cain and Abel.[4] The first text comes from the brief retelling of the biblical story found in the writings of Flavius Josephus, a Jew of the first century of the common era. Here is how he narrates part of the episode in question (*Jewish Antiquities*, 1:53-57).

> Now the brothers enjoyed different pursuits. Abel, the younger one, was concerned with justice, and, believing that God was present at every action that he himself undertook, he made a practice of virtue: he was a shepherd. Cain, however, was altogether wicked, and on the lookout only for his own profit: he was the first person to think of plowing the earth.
>
> Now he killed his brother under these circumstances: They had decided to offer sacrifices to God. Cain brought the produce of the tilled earth and plants, while Abel brought the milk and the firstborn of the flocks. This latter was the sacrifice that God preferred, who is paid homage by whatever grows on its own and in keeping with nature, but not by things brought forth by force and the scheming of greedy man. Then Cain, provoked to anger by the fact that Abel had been shown preference by God, killed his brother and hid his dead body, imagining that he might escape unnoticed. But God, knowing what had been done, came to Cain and inquired as to where indeed his brother might have gone, since he had not seen him for many days, whereas previously he had

---

4. Much has been written on the exegetical history of this story. See in general Aptowitzer, *Kain and Abel*. On the targumic tradition in particular see (inter alia) Vermes, *Post-Biblical Jewish Studies*, 92-126; see also Grelot, "Targums"; Isenberg, "Anti-Sadducee Polemic"; Levine, "Gen. IV:1-6"; and Bassler, "Cain and Abel."

always seen him together with Cain. Cain, at something of a loss
and having nothing to answer to God, at first asserted that he
himself was surprised not to see his brother. But provoked by God's
persistent and meddlesome inquiries, Cain said he was not charged
with taking care of his brother or being his keeper and watching
over his affairs. At this point God declared Cain guilty of having
murdered his brother: "I am astonished," he said, "that you cannot
say what has become of a man whom you yourself have done away
with."

One thing is clear in Josephus's retelling of the biblical story: he
basically believes it is some kind of *lesson*, an instruction in
morality, and has therefore gone to the trouble of characterizing
the difference between the brothers in precisely such terms:
Abel is "concerned with justice" and "the practice of virtue,"
while Cain is "altogether wicked." The biblical account, of
course, says no such thing, and one might think that Josephus
the historian, anxious simply to trace the collected records of
his people from ancient times, would have treated this episode
in bare outline, simply as a glimpse of ancient ancestors
preserved in Israel's literature, devoid of all moralizing
content. But of course this is not his view of the Bible, nor is it
that of any other early Jewish writer.

This is not to say, of course, that he did not find difficulties
in reading this text as a cautionary tale, for in retelling it,
Josephus has gone to some trouble in order to justify God's
actions. In the biblical account, for example, no reason is given
for God's rejection of Cain's sacrifice—one might simply
conclude that God prefers animal sacrifices to vegetable ones on
the basis of taste or smell! But to Josephus and other early
Jewish exegetes, such a conclusion would of course have
seemed quite unlikely, if not blasphemous. And so he has
focused on an otherwise unimportant detail of the story in
order to explain the divine action. For the story mentions that
Cain was a farmer and Abel a shepherd; in the Bible this is
obviously meant to explain why each brother brings the sort of

sacrifice he does. But for Josephus it has additional significance: he associates the brothers' different professions with differences in their character. The fact that Abel is a shepherd bespeaks his concern for proper conduct, the careful guarding of his flock indicating to Josephus an overall concern with virtue. Cain's pursuit of agriculture, on the contrary, is made out to be indicative of his greedy, grasping nature. (What Josephus himself *really* thought about farmers and shepherds is unimportant here; he may have shaped his opinions to fit the narrative.) But the mention of the two brothers' professions was ultimately used by Josephus to justify the fact that God ends up preferring Abel's sacrifice. It is because there is something intrinsically better about offerings from the herd—they arrive "naturally" rather than by the greedy action of plowing the earth to plunder its riches.

In putting forth such an explanation, Josephus has not only succeeded in giving a rational and fair explanation for what otherwise might appear an irrational and unfair act, God's preference for one offering over another; but he has also, as noted, turned the brothers into something like *moral exemplars*, the one a representative of virtuous human beings in general, the other a representative of all that is greedy and grasping. Thus the story of Abel's murder is now played out in an utterly unambiguous fashion. The victim is not only innocent, but virtuous; he is the "good guy," while his murderer is a thoroughgoing villain even before the murder.

There is one other detail worth noting in Josephus's account. He is apparently bothered by the fact that, in the Bible, God is represented as having asked Cain, "Where is your brother Abel?" For such a question might indicate to the ordinary reader that God did not *know* where Abel was, and this conclusion would be further supported by God's later statement that "the voice of your brother's blood is crying to me from the ground"—as if only that sound had indicated to God Abel's whereabouts. None of this, needless to say, squares very well with the picture of divine knowledge presented elsewhere in the Bible, or the one adhered to by Jews like Josephus.

And so, in his retelling of the story, Josephus makes specific mention of God's "knowing what had been done." In fact, Cain's belief that he might escape detection is presented in order to appear foolish and is pointedly contrasted to Abel's conviction, stated right at the beginning of Josephus's retelling, that God is "present at every action." In keeping with this, God's later question about Abel's whereabouts is presented by Josephus as a kind of judicial cross-examination rather than a real question. Indeed, he seems to find some support for this view in our biblical text, for Cain's answer, "I do not know, am I my brother's keeper?" strikes Josephus as really *two* answers— as if Cain had first answered "I do not know," and only later, pressed "by God's persistent and meddlesome inquiries," blurted out a response that showed both his ill will toward his brother and his own lack of remorse: "Am I my brother's keeper?" Having thus trapped Cain in his own words, God then does not hesitate to "declare him guilty" by indicating that he, God, had known about the murder all along.

A MOTIVE FOR MURDER

Why did Cain kill Abel? From the standpoint of a modern biblicist trying to read the story through the eyes of an ancient Israelite, the question of motive is largely irrelevant. The story recounts Cain's rejected sacrifice, and that, presumably, is enough to establish some sort of motive for the killing. If, for the ancient Israelites, the whole point of this tale was to account for the Kenites being what the Israelites knew them to be, then the question of motive was in any case somewhat beside the point. What mattered was that the archetypal "Cain" did in fact kill his brother, had to become a nomad as a result, and ultimately was issued the divine dispensation, "Anyone who kills a Kenite . . ." etc. But of course once this tale becomes part of the divine book of instruction, the question of motive takes on new importance—and so, for example, we saw that Josephus goes out of his way to supply a motive where the Bible has none: "Then Cain, *provoked to anger* by the fact that Abel had been shown preference by God, killed his brother." (In the biblical account, Cain's anger—or better, embarrassment—is mentioned in the sacrifice scene, but nothing is said of his motive for the murder.) But even such an explanation may not have been sufficient to justify the world's first murder in the eyes of some ancient readers, for elsewhere a somewhat stronger motivation is supplied.

The following is the well-known elaboration of this story found in Targum Neophyti, an interpretive translation of the Bible into Aramaic that survives from late antiquity:

> Then [after the incident of the sacrifices] Cain said to his brother Abel, "Come, let us both go out into the field," and it came to pass that when the two had gone into the field Cain cried out to Abel, "It is my view that the world was not created with divine love and is not arranged in keeping with people's good deeds, but justice is corrupted—for why else was your sacrifice accepted with favor and mine not?"
>
> Abel said to Cain: "It is my view that the world was created with divine love and is indeed arranged in keeping with people's good deeds. For it was because my deeds were better than yours that my sacrifice was accepted with favor and your sacrifice was not."
>
> Cain said to Abel, "There is no judgment and no divine judge and no other world [but this one], no reward given to the righteous and no punishment exacted from the wicked."
>
> It was about these matters that the two of them fought in the field and Cain rose up against his brother Abel and killed him.

This retelling of the story takes a radical turn: it supplies an entire conversation not found in the biblical account. For, taking its cue from Gen. 4:8 ("And it came to pass when they were in the field"), the Targum imagines that Cain did not simply up and kill his brother, but was provoked to do so by an argument that developed as the two were strolling along in the field. The argument, though phrased in high theological terms, boils down to a disagreement about why Cain's sacrifice was rejected by God, and the implications of this rejection for each brother's view of the universe. Cain, according to our narrative, feels that the rejection of his sacrifice was entirely arbitrary, and this leads him to conclude that the world in general is run in a cold and ultimately random fashion: sinners are not punished, the righteous are not rewarded, "there is no judgment and no divine judge." Abel (unfortunately for him) feels compelled to disagree. The key to the whole incident, he says to Cain, is our own past history. "My deeds were better than yours," he asserts, and that is why God preferred Abel's sacrifice to Cain's. And far from proving that the universe is randomly ordered, Abel adds, the incident proves that indeed "there is a judgment and a divine judge." Whereupon Cain kills him. (Some early Jewish exegetes even specify here the murder weapon Cain used: he struck his brother with a rock conveniently placed in their path.)

Not only has this retelling fleshed out somewhat the circumstances of Abel's murder, but it has made the sequence of events a bit more plausible. For now we understand why Cain's anger was directed against his brother rather than God: divine rejection was hard enough on poor Cain, but what was intolerable was Abel's attempt to justify that rejection, and to justify it in terms that were certainly insulting and hurtful to Cain. Enraged by Abel's words, Cain could not restrain himself. It should also be remarked that the Targum has, in a manner somewhat similar to Josephus's retelling, sharply characterized the two brothers. In fact, Abel's virtuousness here is not simply asserted, as it was in Josephus, but illustrated: for Abel is the one who believes in divine justice and divine love, whereas Cain, a prototype of the faithless nay-sayer, sneers openly at them. Again, this retelling has turned a somewhat ambiguous biblical tale into a morality play.[5]

Note also that the Targum's retelling presents a somewhat different reason for the divine rejection of Cain's sacrifice. Josephus, for his part, had found a reason intrinsic in the very nature of the two sacrifices: animal offerings were "natural," vegetable offerings "grasping" (though of course this in turn reflected on the characters of the sacrificers). But in the targumic account, it is not so much Cain's and Abel's characters as their past history that makes the difference: quite apart from the sacrifices, Abel's past deeds in general have been good, Cain's bad. Now this in fact works somewhat better than Josephus's explanation. For presumably God might have looked with favor on either offering, or both; but it was because of Abel's life of good deeds, as opposed to Cain's less illustrious history, that the former's sacrifice was accepted and the latter's was not.

ABEL'S "BLOODS"

The traditional Hebrew text of the biblical story contains a slight anomaly; translated literally Gen. 4:10 reads: "And he [the LORD] said: What have you done? Listen, your brother's bloods are crying out to me from the ground." The use of the plural,

5. In fact, the precise opinions expressed by Cain concerning the absence of a last judgment as well as a reward and punishment for deeds done on earth have caused many modern scholars to suppose that Cain, the "villain," is being depicted in order to represent the opinions of one or more religious sects whose views the author of the Targum (and like-minded Jews) opposed. For by attributing to Cain the opinions of a contemporary Sadducee or Epicurean, the Targumist can imply that the point (or at least part of the point) of the Cain and Abel story was that the opinions of these groups have always been wrong, indeed, were precisely those adopted by the world's first villain.

bloods, must have seemed strange to early Jewish interpreters: why use the plural when the singular certainly would have done better?

That this was a question being asked is apparent from the Mishnah, a codification of Jewish law and practice put into final form near the end of the second century C.E. The Mishnah does not generally present much direct interpretation of Scripture. And so it only happens to speak about Cain and Abel in describing the sort of speech a judge should make in warning witnesses in a legal case of the gravity of perjury. This passage is from Tractate Sanhedrin 4:5.

> How were witnesses admonished in capital cases? . . . [They were told:] Keep in mind that capital cases are not like property cases. In property cases, a person [who testifies falsely] can make repayment and atone; but in capital cases, the accused's blood and that of all his potential descendants to the end of time are his [the witness's] responsibility. And so Scripture implies in the case of Cain, who killed his brother; for the text says, "your brother's *bloods* are crying out to me . . ."—not "blood," but "bloods," that is, his blood and that of his potential descendants. Another explanation: "your brother's *bloods*" because his blood had been spattered over tree and stone.

The Mishnah here presents two different explanations for the plural form, explanations that must have been current at the time of its codification. The first is somewhat moralistic. It understands that the Bible uses the word "bloods" in order to teach that someone who takes another person's life is guilty not only of snuffing out that one particular individual, but of destroying all the potential children, grandchildren, great-grandchildren and so forth that might have come from the victim had the murder not taken place. "Bloods," in other words, was understood as indicating that there is never simply one victim, but that (as the Mishnah says elsewhere) "a whole worldfull" of people hangs on each and every human life. Along with this explanation, however, the Mishnah lists another, somewhat more naturalistic one: the plural "bloods" was used to indicate Cain's brutality—he slew his brother in so violent a fashion that there was not merely one pool of blood, but "bloods" spattered over the whole area of the murder.

WHY WAS CAIN EVIL?

Early Christians were of course heir to previous Jewish exegetical traditions, and it is natural that one should find many similarities in their understanding of the story of Cain and Abel. Thus the notion that Abel was not only an innocent victim, but that the story pits good against evil, the "righteous" Abel against the "wicked" Cain, is found in early Christian sources as well: Matt. 23:35 and parallel passages speak of the "righteous blood" of Abel. In a similar vein, 1 John 3:10-12 observes:

> By this it may be seen who are the children of God and who are the children of the devil; whoever does not do right is not of God, nor he who does not love his brother. For this is the message which you have heard from the beginning, that we should love one another, and not be like Cain who was of the evil one and murdered his brother. And why did he murder him? Because his own deeds were evil and his brother's righteous.

For the author of 1 John, the story of Cain has a simple moral: "We should love one another, and not be like Cain." This message is so fundamental that God chose to impart it almost at the very beginning of human history and of the Bible: "You have heard it from the beginning" (cf. 1 John 2:7). Beyond this, the idea that God's reason for rejecting Cain's sacrifice had to do with the nature of the sacrificers is an explanation we have seen above in Targum Neophyti—only here this fact is not only the reason for God's rejection, but the motive for Cain's murder of Abel: he kills him, according to 1 John, "because his own deeds were evil and his brother's righteous."

But 1 John also connects the murder to a somewhat different notion, that Cain was by birth "of the evil one," that is, of the devil. He does not specifically say so, but this idea, too, is based on the biblical text of our story. For in the account of the birth of Cain (Gen. 4:1), Eve is quoted as saying: "I have gotten a man with [the help of] the Lord." Even today, the precise sense of these words in Hebrew is quite mysterious: Why "man," for example, and not "child" or "baby"? And in what sense was the child gotten "with the Lord"? One early Jewish interpretation of these words held that Cain was not the true offspring of Adam, but of some (demonic) heavenly creature.[6] He thus was a "man" (in the sense of "angelic being" that this Hebrew term was sometimes held to have)[7] engendered by one on high (hence, loosely, "with the Lord"). The author of 1 John, knowing this tradition, uses it to bolster his overall contention that "he who commits sin is of the devil" (1 John 3:8). For to him, the story of Cain illustrates as well the enormous gap separating the righteous from the wicked. They belong to two different orders of being.

CAIN AND ABEL TYPOLOGICALLY

As with many stories in the Hebrew Bible, this one was also interpreted by Christians typologically, that is, as a foreshadowing of later things, specifically the events recounted in the Gospels. The killing of Abel, who by now had long since been held to be the "righteous" brother and a paragon of virtue, could not but suggest to early Christians a parallel to the crucifixion. Indeed, the specific mention of Abel's "blood(s)"

6. Witnessed, for example, in Targum Pseudo-Jonathan, ad loc. See A. Goldberg, "Kain."

7. Thus the "man" of Gen. 32:25 was interpreted to mean "angel," as were the three "men" who visit Abraham in Gen. 18:2. Cf. the quasi-divine "man" in Dan. 12:7.

suggested a typological connection to "the sprinkled blood" of Jesus, blood that, to the author of the letter to the Hebrews, "speaks more graciously than the blood of Abel" (Heb. 12:24). This sort of connection continued to fascinate Christians long after the close of the New Testament canon. In particular, as the Jews came to be stigmatized for the death of Jesus, Christians also sought to identify Cain typologically with them. Augustine of Hippo (354-430) adopted such an approach; here is a brief statement of his view of our story (*City of God*, 15:7):

> But Cain took God's commandment [to avoid envy] heedlessly; indeed, as the sin of envy grew overpowering within him, he murdered his brother with malice aforethought. Such was the one who founded the earthly city. However, he also symbolized the Jews, by whom Christ, shepherd of the flocks of men, was killed. [It is Christ] whom Abel, shepherd of the flocks of sheep, prefigures. But since this matter is in a prophetic allegory, I shall not speak of it more here.

For Augustine, Cain's primary significance is as the founder of the "earthly city," but he is also, by a "prophetic allegory" (that is, by typological prefiguration), a foreshadowing of the Jews. Augustine seeks to bolster this identification with another element. It is not only that Abel was murdered and Jesus crucified, but that Abel's profession is specifically said to be shepherding, caring for flocks. To Augustine and other Christians, this could only suggest a foreshadowing of Jesus, who said "I am the good shepherd" (John 10:11). Christian polemic against the Jews, which continued throughout the Middle Ages and beyond, often worked in tandem with this typological identification of the Jews with Cain. For the mysterious "sign" (or "mark" or "brand") given to Cain in Gen. 4:15 had been variously interpreted as a divine letter engraved on Cain's forehead, or divine forgiveness granted as a *sign* to future sinners, or yet others.[8] But the tradition that identified Cain with the demonic sometimes understood the sign to be a set of horns or the like, and these in turn came to figure in the iconographic representation of Jews in medieval art.[9]

ANCIENT EXEGESIS AND MODERN SCHOLARSHIP

On this somewhat sour note, I should like to conclude this brief survey of the Cain and Abel story in early exegesis in order to return to the more general question raised at the outset. For it seems to me that one thing that this little sampling from the history of biblical exegesis may bring into focus is the enormous gap separating not the Jewish Bible from the Christian Old Testament, but ancient exegesis (both Jewish and Christian) on the one side and modern biblical scholarship on the other. Different as they may be, all the ancient exegetes surveyed seem to share certain basic assumptions about the biblical text. They by and large believe that the story of Cain and Abel is a story of good and evil, a bit of instruction whose lessons may therefore find immediate application in the present time. And they are of course convinced that the God who acts in this and other stories is just—so that (for example) if his rejection of Cain's sacrifice might appear to us unfair, they do not hesitate to supply a reason for it. Beyond this (although I have not stressed it heretofore), they believe that this story is part of a divinely given text which is by definition perfect and highly significant, even down to the anomalous plural "bloods." And so the Bible's teachings, while not always apparent on first reading (hence the need for our interpreters and their careful exegesis), ultimately will make themselves known, and this to the great

---

8. The Hebrew word for "sign," אות, came to mean "letter of the alphabet," and was so interpreted by some Jews in relation to our story.

9. See on this Mellinkoff, *Sign of Cain*.

benefit of those who read it, who will find in it a guide to daily life in this world and a way to eternal happiness in the next.

This is not to say, of course, that Jews and Christians had little to disagree about with regard to biblical exegesis in late antiquity. Obviously the typological approach to Scripture reflected in some of the New Testament texts mentioned and later fully developed by such figures as Augustine was not only methodologically foreign to rabbinic exegesis (though some lines of connection nonetheless exist), but its conclusions— here, that Cain and Abel foreshadow the crucifixion—were clearly unacceptable to Jews. But what I wish to stress is simply that underlying these very significant differences are still more significant similarities (explainable by the simple historical circumstance that Christianity originated as a Jewish sect and thus had inherited not only Jewish Scripture but, as well, the main assumptions and methods for understanding Scripture from earlier generations of Jewish exegetes). These similarities emerge in stark dimensions precisely when one juxtaposes ancient Jewish and Christian exegesis en bloc to modern biblical scholarship and its own methods and assumptions.

For it is over against interpretations such as we have just read that the whole movement of modern biblical scholarship arose. Unwilling, or increasingly unable, to view the story of Cain and Abel (and dozens like it) as morality tales, still less as foreshadowings of the New Testament, biblical scholars over the last two or three centuries have come to a radically new approach, some of whose main traits were illustrated by the modern explanations of Cain and Abel with which I began. For modern exegesis starts with an understanding of biblical texts that derives from the historical circumstances in which they arose, making reference (where appropriate) to ancient Israel's neighbors and their writings and beliefs. So, in the modern reading that I have sketched, what is crucial is the historical existence (verifiable from other sources) of an ancient nomadic tribe called the Kenites, as well as the understanding of *etiology* (in the broad sense in which I have used it) as the motive for much of ancient Israel's history writing (as well as that of some of its neighbors). Moreover, individual texts like the Cain and Abel story are basically to be read by modern scholars in contextual isolation, that is, without reference to surrounding material (and certainly without reference to reflections or interpretations of such stories in far distant texts like the New Testament). Indeed, even the unity of a single narrative is not to be taken for granted, since so often in the recent past such narratives have been revealed to be a patchwork of different tellings from different hands in different periods. And in all this the whole question of these stories' divine origin—the most crucial and obvious thing about them for our ancient exegetes—is largely bracketed by all but the modern biblical theologian. On the contrary, biblical texts are explained with reference to human authors and transmitters motivated by wholly human considerations often connected to the precise historical circumstances in which they happened to find themselves.

And so the gulf separating these two basic approaches to Scripture seems to me central. The first sort of approach— harmonistic, often apologetic, frequently fanciful—is generally called "precritical" exegesis nowadays; the second—based on historical knowledge and scientific method—is today's critical or historical biblical scholarship. And, as we have seen, they produce quite different results, the modern scholar's reconstruction of the Israelite view of their neighboring Kenites vs. the morality tale of Cain and Abel. The modern is "fact," the other, "fable." The modern—so it is often conceived—is a reflection of the "text itself," rooted in the time of its origin; the

other is interpretation of the freest sort, belonging to a time
centuries after the story was first told.

These differences are, I think, paradigmatic, and express
much of the dilemma of the Bible in the modern world. For of
course the story of Cain and Abel, understood according to the
interpretation we have labelled "fact," is largely irrelevant to
the Bible as a religious text, as the Scripture of Judaism and
Christianity. But Cain and Abel the "fable" is equally
problematic to moderns, or at least to those schooled in the
ways of modern biblical scholarship, who find themselves
unable to accept the typological reading of Scripture, or indeed
many of the main traits of ancient exegesis illustrated in our
examples, as a true representation of what these biblical texts
were first intended to communicate. And so we moderns are
stuck. Even if we were inclined to try to do away with the new
biblical science and return to Cain and Abel the fable, the sound
of Gunkel's "bloods" would inexorably rise out of the ground,
and its faint but persistent whimper, "Etiology, etiology!",
would trouble our exegetical peace.

THE ORAL TORAH

Having identified this dilemma as the crucial issue, in my
opinion, for both Jews and Christians in biblical scholarship, I
hesitate even to approach the subject of a possible solution for
one or both groups. I hesitate in particular because much has
already been written on this complicated topic, and there is
little of value that I can hope to add now in a few brief pages.
Nevertheless, it seems imperative in this context to say at least
a few words, and that in particular with reference to traditional
Jewish belief.

For I daresay that the only solution of which I can conceive
is, from the standpoint of rabbinic Judaism, hardly new. It is
clear that the Rabbis who lived during, or just after, the

flowering of rabbinic Judaism were, in some ways, in a position identical to our own. They, too, had inherited traditions about the meaning of the biblical text that, in their own eyes, sometimes contradicted the plain meaning of the words, common sense, or common practice. And so their reaction to this situation (or indeed, the similar reaction of later generations of Jewish exegetes) is instructive. They essentially granted to the inherited traditions an authority of their own and established them as coequal to the biblical text itself. Thus, there exists an authoritative body of tradition, an oral Torah, that interprets and applies the written one (that is, the Bible) in definitive fashion, and this oral teaching, whose origins are traced back to the time of Moses himself, required therefore that the Bible not be freely interpreted, each exegete doing what was proper in his own eyes, but that each new generation of explainers follow in the footsteps of those who had preceded them. Indeed, the same was basically true of the early Church, where authority was vested not in the biblical text alone, but in the Church and in its learned doctors, who had laid the foundations of Christian teaching and established the broad lines of scriptural interpretation for generations to come.

I might say that, from the standpoint of a cold-blooded biblicist, there is nonetheless a certain historical validity to such an approach. For one thing that the last three or four decades of biblical scholarship have made abundantly clear is that the "fable" understanding of ancient Israelite texts is one that itself is well-rooted within the biblical period—that is, centuries before the Bible itself existed as a defined corpus of sacred texts, some of its parts already were being interpreted in ways wholly out of keeping with the original meaning and intention of their authors. This "fabulous" reading of Cain and Abel and other stories constituted a sort of second authorship for these tales: retold and radically altered by their interpreters, they were in a sense written anew even before they became part of something called the Bible. And so one might well conclude that our Bible never did just consist of the naked words of the text on the page, but of those words as they had already been definitively and authoritatively interpreted of old. The Bible of the Jews is, ultimately, the Bible of the Rabbis, interpreted and explained in the pages of the Babylonian Talmud and other rabbinic works, and elaborated by later commentators in consonance with those earlier interpretations; and similarly, the Bible of the Christians is the Bible of the Church, the source of Christian doctrine as it had been passed on and elaborated from the Church's beginning.

To view things in this fashion may seem only to beg the main issue of biblical interpretation; if we hold these texts to be sacred and to derive their authority ultimately from divine revelation, then can we so blithely allow their first authorship (presumably the divine one) to be subsumed, perhaps perverted, by their second authorship (even if the latter was in fact the one that produced the document eventually canonized by synagogue and church)? I should readily concede that this is a difficult question, and one that I cannot even begin to address in the present context. But I would point out that the issue ultimately must turn not on any facile distinction between divine and human texts, but on one's very notion of the nature of scriptural inspiration and authority: What does it mean to hold a text to be the word of God? And since this is an idea whose presence in many of the biblical texts to which it is imputed is hardly obvious from the texts' own words, it therefore turns out to be, often at least, just one more item whose very existence is not part of the text itself, but only arrived as part the Bible's second authorship.

Nor, I might add in closing, is this a problem to which rabbinic authors were insensitive, and if the solution to which they adhered—essentially, to claim that authoritative interpretation was itself divinely inspired—is not, perhaps, surprising, the formulation through which this doctrine was communicated certainly was. Particularly striking is the following, which is attributed to the third-century rabbinic scholar R. Isaac, and is presented, appropriately, in the form of an interpretive comment upon the introduction to the Decalogue (Exod. 20:1): "And God spoke all these words, saying . . . ."[10]

> That which the prophets were later to prophesy in every subsequent age, they received here at Mount Sinai. For thus did Moses report to Israel (Deut. 29:13-14) "Not with you alone do I make this covenant . . . but with those who are standing here among us today, and with those who are not here among us today." Now it is not written "not *standing* among us today," but only "not here among us today": for these were the souls that were yet to be created, who had no substance, and of whom "standing" could not be said. For though they did not exist at the time, every one of these received his portion. . . . And not only did all the prophets receive their prophecies from Sinai, but also the sages [that is, interpreters] who were to arise in every generation—each of them received his [teaching] from Sinai, as it is written, "These are the words the Lord spoke to all your assembly on the mountain amid the fire, the cloud and the darkness, with a great noise, *and did not cease.*"

---

10. The passage, from Exodus Rabbah 28:6 (cf. Midrash Tanḥuma, Yitro 11) specifically addresses the apparently emphatic "God spoke *all* these words," as well as perhaps the word *saying* (לאמר), which was regularly understood by rabbinic exegetes as meaning "to say later on."

Humanity in God's Image: Rabbinic Biblical Theology and Genesis 1:26-28

ROGER BROOKS

The creation of humankind in God's image (Genesis 1:26-27) represents a foundational element of the biblical message:

> Then God said, "I'll make humanity [אדם] in my image and likeness. They will rule over fish in the sea, birds in the heavens, cattle, the entire earth, even over the creepy things that crawl on the ground." So God created humanity [האדם] in his own image—he created it in God's image: he created them as male and female.

That passage takes up a standard problem facing religious traditions, namely, What is the essence of humanity? The Bible answers in a self-confident manner: we are divine, or at least like the Deity. I cannot image how anyone who penned this verse, with its optimistic notion of human nature, could ever think that all humans are *by definition* evil. Little wonder, then, that the biblical narrative finds a place for humankind's sin and expulsion from the Garden of Eden. Their creation alone would not allow one to predict that people could be as bad as they are.

In my remarks on this passage, I will not focus on philology or considerations of the intricate details of language, syntax, gender, and the like. To my mind, these issues do not go to the core of rabbinic theology. Neither do such investigations allow this single passage to exemplify something broader beyond itself.[1] Rather, my goal is to show how a central and elementary aspect of the rabbinic worldview—a vision that undergirds almost all of Judaism even to our own day—emerges out of a particular reading of the *Tanakh*.

At the foundation of most rabbinic thought and law lies an interesting coordination. God and humanity are taken as partners in life, together participating in each turn of affairs, each deed, each act. That coordination finds implicit expression throughout rabbinic literature. For what Israelites do and how they act must concord with the categories laid down at creation; if not, the actions simply are invalid or prohibited. Examples of this coordination are well known: Jews must eat "ordinary foods"—fish that swim (that is, with fins and scales), but not those that walk in the water (like lobsters or crabs); animals that resemble pastoral cattle (that is, cloven-hooved ruminants).[2] In his work on the Temple and its requirements of purity, Jacob Neusner points up the same coordination between human activity and God's creation: people recently in contact with the dead (that is, suffering corpse uncleanness) cannot approach the source of life (that is, the Temple).[3] To violate the Temple in this manner would be an abomination of the divine gift. These examples show how categories laid out originally in the Hebrew Bible then are taken over by the community, and become definitive of the way Jews live their lives.

Matters extend at least one step further in this parallel world between what God has created and what humans must do. In the Genesis story, humanity validates God's creation by naming things. In rabbinic thought, by corrolary, God validates

---

1. Note as well that I do not carry out an examination of the midrashic treatment of Gen. 1:26-27, with its description of the heavenly court, and the like.

2. See Douglas, *Purity and Danger*, 54-57.

3. See Neusner, "History and Structure," 101-31, esp. pp. 126-27.

human affairs when the correct wording or procedure is followed. The scribal aspect of rabbinism here is in full force: what Jews commit to paper in the proper manner, or what they recite from paper in the proper manner, can invoke God's approval. Examples again are easy to come by: writs of marriage and divorce function to create or dissolve heavenly bonds, because of the precision of their language. Anyone who has ever witnessed or been present as a rabbinic court draws up a divorce decree (גט) can testify to just how precise this language must be. It is rare for a divorce to be effected without several copies of the decree started, found to be invalid, then ripped up and thrown out.

The key to the coordination between the divine and human realms thus is twofold.

First, God's activity in creating the world day-by-day demands human action in response (a response encapsulated within the legal categories of the Mishnah, edited around 200 C.E., and later rabbinic law codes). God's ownership of the land of Israel affects how Israelites may use that land and its produce. God's interaction with Israel in history orients the whole calendar and marks out special times requiring special actions. The sanctity demanded by God of the Israelites affects their relationships within the family unit and especially the relationship between men and women. The unity and equality of God's holy people, Israel, demands special action in business, government, and day-to-day dealings. The worship of God demands special action in the Temple. Extending the holiness required in the Temple to everyday life demands, in turn, special attention to all aspects of life with respect to cultic purity.

Second, in reacting to God's activity, the human will or intention matters in the larger scheme of things. Not only does what God demands of humanity make a difference, but how people respond makes a difference. What Israelites want and intend demands God's attention. Neusner cogently expresses the matter:

> The Mishnah's Judaism is a system built to celebrate that power of [hu]man[s] to form intention, willfully to make the world with full deliberation, in entire awareness, through decision and articulated intent. So does the Mishnah assess the condition of Israel, defeated and helpless, yet in its Land: without power, yet holy; lacking all focus, in no particular place, certainly without Jerusalem, yet set apart from the nations.[4]

Judaism in its rabbinic mode—the only Judaism with which we have any real acquaintance (other than Christianity, perhaps)—relies upon the vision of the priestly writer of the *Tanakh*. Throughout Leviticus, we have painstaking attention to detail of rite, meticulous adherence to categories affecting the Temple cult, and scrupulous care for human relationships. That same writer penned and edited the early accounts of creation under discussion here. So we find in Genesis chapter 1 an ordered and perfect use of the divine will. In creating the world, it was God (by definition) who constructed the categories by which we understand reality: light and dark; day and night; fish and fowl; cattle and humans; the list goes on and on.

But then God turns to the first earthling (האדם) to name these creations. It is the earthling—Adam—who gives each animal its title and so finishes God's creative act. God arranges matter, then calls upon humanity to package creation neatly and to seal it. From the very first chapter of the *Tanakh*, then, these two essentially separate realms are brought into coordination: the Divine realm and its mirror complement, the human realm. In somewhat more theological terms, God creates, but leaves it to humanity to sanctify: "Life," in the Jewish religion, "consists of endless opportunities to sanctify

---

4. Neusner, *Judaism: The Evidence of the Mishnah*, 283.

the profane, opportunities to redeem the power of God from the chain of potentialities, opportunities to serve spiritual ends."[5]

So it is that Judaism as a religion is concerned with sanctification, attaining salvation only through that means. The creation account, especially its depiction of humans in God's image and likeness, lies at the heart of what makes Judaism, Judaism. God has created the opportunities that confront us; we must respond within a world of perfect order to enliven and sanctify ourselves.

Now the categories and parameters within which this action takes place constitute Jewish Law (הלכה), the way of life. In other words, part and parcel of God's creation of the world was the creation of the legal system (since it is categorically rooted in the creation story). It is humanity's task to live within that legal framework established at creation by God, in whose image we continue to exist.

Howard Eilberg-Schwartz sums up this theological assertion, basic to rabbinism:

> The capacity to think . . . makes human beings like God . . . . From the sages' standpoint, "being made in God's image" means being able to exercise one's mind in the same way that God exercises the divine will . . . . From the Mishnah's standpoint, human beings are endowed with powers similar to God's, because they have the capacity to carry out the same intellectual operations as God . . . .[6]

The Jewish people thus are caught up in a never-ending pattern of *imitatio dei*. So long as they continue to act in the world of *halakhah*, they are bound to the role of God's complement. Let us not forget that God, too, according to rabbinic legend, is responsible for performing the commandments; God wears *tefillin* every morning; God studies Torah according to rabbinic

5. See Heschel, *God in Search of Man*, 291.
6. Eilberg-Schwartz, *Human Will in Judaism*, 182-83.

principles. Just as from creation humanity exists in God's image and is obliged to imitate God, so, according to Jewish theology, God continues to model that proper behavior by adhering to Jewish Law.

The Historical-Critical and Feminist Readings of Genesis 1:26-28

ADELA YARBRO COLLINS

When a historical critic approaches a text, the governing question is what the text meant in its original context. Consider Gen. 1:26-28:

> And God said: "Let us make humankind (האדם) in our image, after our likeness; and let them have dominion over the fish of the sea, over the birds of the heavens, over the domestic animals, over all the earth, and over every creeping thing that creeps upon the earth." And God created humankind (האדם) in his image; in the image of God created he him; male and female created he them.[1]

Historical critics have asked what the author intended by the phrases translated "in the image of God" (בצלם אלהים) and "in [God's] image" (בצלמו). Recently, Phyllis Bird has articulated the consensus:

- Verse 27 may not be interpreted in isolation; in other words, discussions of the meaning of the "image of God" should take verses 26-28 as the unit, not just verses 26-27.
- The theme of sexual distinction and reproduction is to be dissociated from the theme of the divine image and the theme of dominion.

---

1. See Trible, *God and the Rhetoric of Sexuality*, 12-13.

- The theme of sexual distinction and reproduction belongs
  to the larger theme of fertility and sustainability in the
  general context.[2]

The purpose of humankind, according to Genesis chapter 1, is
to rule over the realm of the creatures. This rule is made
possible by the divine stamp that sets this creature apart from
the rest and identifies it as God's representative. The "likeness"
between humanity and God lies in the corresponding activities
of "having dominion." Thus, "image of God" is a royal
designation. This inference from the context is supported by
evidence from Mesopotamia, close to the Priestly Writer in
language, conception, and time. In three texts cited by Bird, an
identical cognate expression is used as a designation of the king.
The Priestly Writer thus extended to all human beings the
honorary epithet previously reserved for the king.

From this point of view, the mention of sexual
differentiation prepares for the blessing regarding the increase
of the species. Such differentiation is assumed for the other
creatures, but must be mentioned here because of the
immediately preceding statement that humanity is in the
image of God. The idea of God having any quality
corresponding to sexuality or sexual differentiation would have
been utterly foreign to the Priestly Writer. Unlike God but like
the other creatures, humanity has sexuality and sexual
distinction.

In striking contrast to the historical-critical consensus,
Phyllis Trible argues that the sexuality of humankind in Gen.
1:27 pertains to the divine image. The animal world shares
procreation with humanity, but not sexuality.[3] By "sexuality,"
Trible does not refer to the biological level of meaning but to

2. See Bird, "'Male and Female,'" 129-59.
3. Trible, *God and the Rhetoric of Sexuality*, 15.

gender, to sexuality as a system of symbols. The shifts from singular ("humankind," האדם) to plural ("male and female he created them," זכר ונקבה ברא אותם) indicate that from the beginning humankind existed as two creatures, not one creature with a double sex. Further, the singular "humankind" and its singular pronoun show that the two sexes are not opposite but rather harmonious. And the parallelism between "humankind" and "male and female" indicates that sexual differentiation does not mean hierarchy. Created simultaneously and in the image of God, male and female are equal. Neither has power over the other; both are given equal power.

There is evident tension between the historical-critical consensus and at least this particular feminist reading. If one wishes to discern the meaning of the text in the sixth century B.C.E., the historical-critical evidence and analysis must be normative. But Phyllis Trible, like other feminists, is attempting to articulate the significance of the text for women and men in her time and place. Her project is similar to the adaptations of the text carried out by the rabbis and the theologians of the early Church for their times and places.

The Suffering Servant:
Isaiah Chapter 53 as a Christian Text

ADELA YARBRO COLLINS

In the current form of the Roman Catholic liturgy for Good Friday, the fourth Servant Song (Isa. 52:13-53:12) appears as the first reading from Scripture.

> Behold, my servant shall prosper, he shall be exalted and lifted up, and shall be very high.
> As many were astonished at him [you]—his appearance was so marred, beyond human semblance, and his form beyond that of the sons of men—
> so shall he [startle] many nations; kings shall shut their mouths because of him;
> for that which has not been told them they shall see, and that which they have not heard they shall understand.
>
> Who has believed what we have heard? And to whom has the arm of the Lord been revealed?
> For he grew up before him like a young plant, and like a root out of the dry ground;
> he had no form or comeliness that we should look at him, and no beauty that we should desire him.
> He was despised and rejected by men; a man of sorrows, and acquainted with grief;
> and as one from whom men hide their faces he was despised, and we esteemed him not.

Surely he has borne our griefs and carried our sorrows; yet we
    esteemed him stricken, smitten by God, and afflicted.
But he was wounded for our transgressions, he was bruised for our
    iniquities;
upon him was the chastisement that made us whole, and with his
    stripes we are healed.

All we like sheep have gone astray; we have turned every one to
    his own way;
and the Lord has laid on him the iniquity of us all.

He was oppressed, and he was afflicted, yet he opened not his
    mouth;
like a lamb that is led to slaughter, like a ewe that before its
    shearers is dumb,
so he opened not his mouth.
By oppression and judgment he was taken away; and as for his
    generation, who considered
that he was cut off out of the land of the living, stricken for the
    transgression of my people?
And they made his grave with the wicked, and with a rich man in
    his death,
although he had done no violence and there was no deceit in his
    mouth.

Yet it was the will of the Lord to bruise him; he has put him to
    grief;
when he makes himself [you make him] an offering for sin, he shall
    see his offspring, he shall prolong his days;
the will of the Lord shall prosper in his hand;
he shall see the fruit of the travail of his soul and be satisfied; by
    his knowledge shall the righteous one, my servant,
make many to be accounted righteous; and he shall bear their
    iniquities.
Therefore I will divide him a portion with the great, and he shall
    divide the spoil with the strong;
because he poured out his soul to death, and was numbered with the
    transgressors;
yet he bore the sin of many, and made intercession for the
    transgressors.

The use of this passage in the lectionary is based on the traditional Christian interpretation of the Servant Songs of Isaiah, in which the servant is identified with Jesus of Nazareth. The descriptions of the mistreatment and suffering of the servant here and in Isa. 50:6 are seen as prophecies of the passion of Jesus: the arrest, torture, mocking, and crucifixion described in the Gospels of the New Testament.

A common assumption among Christian exegetes has been that the followers of Jesus understood his death in terms of the fourth Servant Song from the very beginning of reflection on the meaning of that death. Historical-critical studies have put this assumption in doubt. In the New Testament, only two passages composed before 70 C.E. contain certain references to the poem, both found in Paul's letter to the Romans. The first citation occurs in the discussion of the relation of Israel to the gospel (Romans chapters 9-11). The immediate context is a discussion of the Christian proclamation and the various responses to it. Paul comments, "But they have not all obeyed the gospel; for Isaiah says, 'Lord, who has believed what he has heard from us?'" (Rom. 10:16, citing the Old Greek of Isa. 53:1). In light of later tradition, it is suprising that this, the oldest clear citation of the fourth Servant Song, is not related to the passion of Jesus.

The other citation in Romans occurs in the personal remarks near the end of the letter (Rom. 15:14-32). In this context Paul states that it has been his "ambition to preach the gospel, not where Christ has already been named, lest I build on another man's foundation, but as it is written, 'They shall see who have never been told of him, and they shall understand who have never heard of him'" (Rom. 15:21, citing the Old Greek translation of Isa. 52:15). Once again, the application of the fourth Servant Song is to the early Christian mission, not to the death of Jesus.

None of the alleged allusions to Isaiah chapter 53 in the Gospel of Mark are indisputable. Matthew has one certain citation. Following the Sermon on the Mount, Matthew narrates three healings. After the third comes a summary of Jesus' healing activity that is based on a similar summary in Mark. Matthew has added to the summary the comment, "This was to fulfill what was spoken of by the prophet Isaiah, 'He took our infirmities and bore our diseases'" (Matt. 8:17, citing Isa. 53:4 in a form other than the Old Greek). Here the Song is applied to the life of Jesus, but to the mighty deeds, not to the passion.

The oldest Christian text that clearly cites the fourth Servant Song in relation to the passion is the Gospel of Luke. The Lucan account of the Last Supper contains a brief dialogue about two swords (Luke 22:35-38). This passage may have been added to explain how it was that a disciple of Jesus had a sword at the time of the arrest in Gethsemane. In any case, Jesus is portrayed as saying, "For I tell you that this scripture must be fulfilled in me, 'And he was reckoned with transgressors'; for what is written about me has its fulfillment" (Luke 22:37, citing Isa. 53:12 in a form very close to the Old Greek). Even though the Song is related to the execution of Jesus, it is not used to explain the significance of Jesus' death. Rather it suggests that his treatment as an insurrectionist or criminal was foreordained.

It is unlikely, however, that the fourth Servant Song was first interpreted by early Christians in the ways just discussed and only later used to understand Jesus' death as vicarious suffering. It is more likely that the identification of Jesus with the Servant, and his passion with the Servant's suffering, was primary. Thus the other uses are best seen as elaborations or extensions of that early interpretation. The pre-Pauline summary of the gospel in 1 Cor. 15:3-4 may be based in part on the Song. The claim that "Christ died for our sins in accordance with the scriptures" (1 Cor. 15:3) may be based on an interpretation of Isa. 53:5-6 in the Old Greek translation: "But he was wounded on account of our sins, and was bruised because of our iniquities . . . and the Lord gave him up for our sins." Similarly, the pre-Pauline hymn cited in Philippians chapter 2 may have been inspired in part by the Song. The idea that Christ "took the form of a servant" (δουλος) may be based on his identification with God's servant (παις) in Isa. 52:13. If the clause "became obedient unto death" (Phil. 2:8) was part of the pre-Pauline hymn, the fourth Servant Song would be a more likely prototype than the other Songs. The contrast between humiliation and exaltation in the Christian hymn may echo the analogous contrast in the fourth Song. In fact the pattern of high/low/high that we find in the Christian hymn may echo the analogous sequence in the Song: "behold, my servant shall understand, and be exalted, and glorified exceedingly" (Isa. 52:13; cf. Phil 2:6—"in the form of God"); "in his humiliation his judgment was taken away" (Isa. 53:8; cf. Phil 2:8—"he humbled himself"); "therefore he shall inherit many, and he shall divide the spoils of the mighty" (Isa. 53:12; cf. Phil 2:9-11—"therefore God has highly exalted him").

One of the most intriguing possibilities regarding the early Christian reading of the fourth Song is that the older text generated narrative developments in the passion account. If the concordance or typology between the Servant of the fourth Song and Jesus was early and presupposed in the development of the passion narrative, then details in the older text may have inspired minor elaborations in the newer text. For example, the image of the Servant "opening not his mouth" and being "led as a sheep to the slaughter," and being "dumb as a lamb before the shearer" (Isa. 53:7) may have evoked the portrayal of Jesus remaining silent and answering nothing to the high priest (Mark 14:61; cf. Matt. 27:12, 14). The prophetic remark, "he was numbered among the transgressors" (Isa. 53:12), may have generated the portrait of Jesus crucified between two robbers or bandits (Mark 15:27; Matt. 27:38). Likewise, the depiction of Jesus praying for those who crucified him and his promise to the repentant criminal in Luke may have been inspired by the comment that the Servant "made intercession for the transgressors" (compare Luke 23:34, 39-43 with Isa. 53:12; the motif of intercession is not in the Old Greek translation).

The ethics of interpretation has many facets. I would like to mention one. As we all know, the passion narratives in the canonical Gospels are easily read in a way that blames the Jewish people for the death of Jesus. Even though his death brought salvation, Christians have sometimes affirmed "Woe to those by whom that death came." And, perhaps misled by the evangelists, they have minimized Pilate's role. The Christian reading of the fourth Servant Song is less conducive to anathematizing one's enemies and to the social injustice that often follows. The powerful poetry is full of mystery, not the least of which is the role of the Deity in all this. In any case, if any blame is to be laid on anyone, it is on the "we" and the "us" of the text with whom the Christian audience identifies.

A Christological Suffering Servant?
The Jewish Retreat into
Historical Criticism

ROGER BROOKS

The Suffering Servant passage, when read christologically, is an ideal test case for joint work between Jews and Christians. Such interpretation, from the beginnings of the Christian movement to our own day, presents a reading that Jews simply cannot tolerate. That is to say, the *Tanakh* cannot speak of Jesus' status as God's servant, of his death and resurrection, or of his messianic mission. If it did, the Jewish reader would have to accept the Christian myth of the passion and resurrection, because God's own revealed words indicate for the myth a role in salvation history.

The most interesting aspect of this question is thus methodological: in ecumenical settings, what happens when Jews are confronted with a reading of the Hebrew Bible they cannot countenance on theological grounds? In such cases, what often occurs is a retreat into historical or literary criticism; Jewish scholars or exegetes use these tools to prevent farfetched readings of Scripture, even as they might (or might not) recognize the awesome problems that would arise if those same critical tools were applied to Jewish interpretations.

GETTING OUR STORIES STRAIGHT: AN UNINTENDED RETREAT

A perfectly good example of this retreat into historical criticism is found in Michael Goldberg's *Getting our Stories Straight: The Exodus and the Passion-Resurrection.* Goldberg spells out the two communities' different master stories (based on the early chapters of Exodus and the opening chapter of Matthew). He neatly shows how each master story makes perfect sense of the world from a certain point of view. But then, in firing what was (I gather) an unintended shot at the Christian master story, Goldberg makes the crucial foray into historical criticism: "Having now attempted to give both narratives an honest and attentive hearing, we are at last in a position to sum up our conclusions as a fair and thoughtful audience." He goes on to summarize the two stories—that is beside the point for now—and then invokes the category of *general historicity*:

> The truth of narratives is to be found . . . through their reference to a whole world of possible relations, a world which the story constantly puts before our imaginations, impelling us to wonder whether its depicted universe *is* reasonably imaginable given the kind of universe with which we human beings are familiar. . . .

Goldberg then speaks directly of Matthew:

> Matthew's picture of a world whose affairs are so completely under God's own sure guidance seems completely foreign and unwarranted, for from our own acquaintance with the course of world affairs, we can see no clear-cut course at all. We might even be inclined to say that such "Mattheanisms" as "all this took place to fulfill what the Lord had spoken by the prophet" (Matt. 1:22), rather than strengthening the plausibility of Matthew's account, only weaken it by making its story line seem not genuinely believable, but instead extremely *plotted*; rather than artfully rendering a reality linking Jesus' story to Israel's, such pointed scriptural references

perhaps end up making Matthew's narrative seem incredibly *artificial*.[1]

Goldberg undertakes no parallel exercise to debunk the Jewish master story. This I take to be evidence, in a small way, of a common tack in modern Jewish-Christian encounters regarding scriptural interpretation. Jews can respond, on historical or historical-critical grounds: "Your reading simply doesn't make sense!"

THE SUFFERING SERVANT IN HISTORICAL AND LITERARY CONTEXT

The retreat into critical reading of the Bible characterizes not only modern Jewish and Christian encounters, but also is part of an old interpretive legacy. In the case of the Servant Songs, the Jewish rejection of any christological reading of is straightforwardly based on historical-literary critical principles.

First, consider the literary context of the biblical text, the style of the author, linguistic usage, etc.: the broader context of Isaiah chapters 40-55 makes it perfectly clear that Second Isaiah and the four Servant Songs address not Jesus but Israel as a whole. Such titles as the Chosen One, the Despised One, and the Wounded One refer not to Jesus, but to Jacob and the whole people of Israel.

The greatest of all Jewish exegetes, Rashi (fl. 1040-1105 C.E.), in his commentary on Isa. 53:3 refers directly to Christian interpretations, and employs just this type of literary criticism: "'He was despised and rejected by men' (Isa. 53:3): The practice of this prophet is to refer to all of Israel as a single man [as in the following, Isa. 44:2]: 'Fear not, My servant Jacob!'" The implication is that, although some might wish to speak in behalf of a messianic interpretation of the Servant, most Jews

---

1. Goldberg, *Getting Our Stories Straight*, 220-21.

and most biblical scholars understand the servant in a collective manner: Israel, Jerusalem, or some remnant of the people.

Second, and even more basic, is this historical-critical presumption: a valid reading of a biblical text must have made sense both to those who penned it and to those who might have read it. And in the time when Second Isaiah was written—the middle of the sixth century B.C.E.—who could have understood anything whatsoever about Jesus?

Divine Love Poetry: The Song of Songs

CHARLES KANNENGIESSER

The first chapter of the Song of Songs is an apt text for a common Jewish and Christian reading, mainly because it reminds us of the closeness between Jewish and Christian exegesis at a time when the two traditions were still able to share their religious values despite antagonistic self-affirmations.

The Song of Songs, which is Solomon's.

O that you would kiss me with the kisses of your mouth!
For your love is better than wine, your anointing oils are fragrant,
   your name is oil poured out; therefore do the maidens love you.
Draw me after you, let us make haste. The king has brought me into
   his chambers.
We will exult and rejoice in you; we will extol your love more than
   wine; rightly do they love you.

I am very dark, but comely, O daughters of Jerusalem, like the tents
   of Kedar, like the curtains of Solomon.
Do not gaze at me because I am swarthy, because the sun has
   scorched me.
My mother's sons were angry with me, they made me keeper of the
   vineyards; but, my own vineyard I have not kept!

Tell me, you whom my soul loves, where you pasture your flock,
   where you make it lie down at noon; for why should I be like
   one who wanders beside the flocks of your companions?
If you do not know, O fairest among women, follow in the tracks of
   the flock, and pasture your kids beside the shepherd's tents.

I compare you, my love, to a mare of Pharaoh's chariots.
Your cheeks are comely with ornaments, your neck with strings of
    jewels.
We will make you ornaments of gold, studded with silver.

While the king was on his couch, my nard gave forth its fragrance.
My beloved is to me a bag of myrrh, that lies between my breasts.
My beloved is to me a cluster of henna blossoms in the vineyards of
    En-gedi.

Behold, you are beautiful, my love; behold, you are beautiful; your
    eyes are doves.
Behold you are beautiful, my beloved, truly lovely.
Our couch is green; the beams of our house are cedar, our rafters are
    pine.

The long commentary and the homilies on the Song of Songs written by Origen of Alexandria in the third century C.E. illustrate a line of thought common to rabbinic and ecclesiastical exegesis. The Song, a beautiful poem, is a symbolic description of the relationship between God and the community of believers. Lover and beloved express in erotic terms the many tensions, happy or not, of the inner encounter with God. Their love affair becomes an allegory of the experience of faith.

That such an allegory could be applied in the same way by Origen and by his Jewish contemporaries to their reciprocal religious institutions presupposes a common understanding of the Song of Songs, even if Origen knew little or nothing about the proper establishment of rabbinic authority in Jewish communities. Rather, the common ground was provided to the separate traditions by shared past foundations. Christianity had become hellenized in its language and in its entire self-understanding. It remained nevertheless *Jewish* in its fundamental assumptions concerning the nature of salvific relationships between God and people called to faith. In the words of Ephraim E. Urbach:

Origen was familiar with contemporary Jewish exegesis, and he
was interested in two aspects of it. In his historical exegesis Origen
follows entirely in the footsteps of Jewish interpretation, and it is
easy to point to parallels; but even in the mystic-spiritual
exposition Jewish elements are to be found. . . .

At times Origen had need only to transcribe the homilies of the
Sages and change a few of their concepts in order to find in them
what he wanted, but such is his pleasure upon discovering an
exposition of this nature that he does not lightly let it go. . . .

Origen uses the ingredients of the midrashic expositions in
order to defend the Church. . . . The impression [that Origen's
homilies are in fact part of a live dialogue with rabbinic
interpreters] grows even stronger when we compare the style and
form of [a] passage . . . with [its] continuation, wherein he collected
a large number of verses in which he found references to the Church
of the Gentiles.[1]

Illustrated in these exerpts is a situation in which religious
culture allowed intellectual leaders of the Christian movement
and of the synagogue to exchange concepts in order to interpret
the relevance, the actual meaning for their tradition and for
their community, of the Song of Songs. Without pretending to
materialize the affinities, it nonetheless is quite clear that on
both sides the situation is the same.

In Origen's case, God of course is identified with Christ, the
believing community with the Church of his time, and the
whole set of dialogues and poems in the Song of Songs became
an allegory for analyzing all different aspects in this partnership
between God and the Christian community. In Origen too, as in
rabbinic exegesis of the time, the individual believer also is
seen as a partner of God. Despite different institutionalizations
and different positions, what is remarkable is the structural
similarities in these symbolic exegeses.

The identification of the loving words and behavior of the
lover to the beloved as expressions of divine revelation moves

---

1. Urbach, "Homiletical Interpretations of the Sages ," 252, 258, and 263-65.

beyond such similarities and is proper to Origen himself. He utilizes the Song of Songs in explaining that the divine lover, in educating us as believers, merely follows the encyclopedic curriculum of the university. He identifies different wisdom books along these lines: Proverbs first of all is a training in ethics; Ecclesiastes deals with physics; the Song of Songs, properly, represents theology or metaphysics, and the Song's most intimate images suggest what is the deepest insight of the believer into God.

As trinitarian theory comes into the picture, we have interpretations of the Song of Songs that reflect the whole culture and respond directly to the needs of a believing community. For Origen, such an understanding was so well attuned to his community that his homilies on the Song of Songs, as well as his commentaries, became popular immediately and had enormous influence in later periods. So, even among those who combated Origen's theoretical a prioris, as for example Bishop Methodius in the beginning of the fourth century in a work entitled *The Symposium* (or *On Virginity*), Origen's commentary is fully represented and used tacitly all around. In the Latin culture, the same commentary tradition spread over into Ambrose of Milan, in his three *Treatises on Virginity*. Ambrose's long commentaries on Psalm 118 take over whole parts of Origen's commentaries; and they became the equivalent of best sellers in the monasteries of Latin medieval times after Bernard of Clairvaux reiterated Origen's enterprise and adjusted it to medieval piety. The single technique of interpretation and the basic insight about the allegorical meaning of the Song of Songs thus spanned many centuries and brought a uniform sense to the Christian tradition.

If we speculate about today, what could the Song of Songs mean now? Think of the fact that we have said goodbye to all our traditions of interpretations past, now that we no longer have God, no longer have Church, no longer have Trinity, no longer have a doctrine of Grace in the present civilization. We must understand such a text in a nondogmatic way. Perhaps one possible interpretation would be to claim that precisely the Song of Songs, as found in the collection of biblical writings, is thoroughly secular. It gives us wonderful language for understanding how strictly secular realities might be infused with religion. Perhaps this is what Dietrich Bonhoeffer meant in one of the letters he wrote from prison when he insisted that the Song of Songs and other Old Testament writings are the best guides to lead one to be a believer in a nonreligious age.

The Song of Songs in Comparative Perspective

ADELA YARBRO COLLINS

The Jewish and Christian allegorical reading of the love poetry of the Song of Songs is not unique in the history of religions. The notion of the Lord as Lover is a mood of devotion in India as old as the Vedic hymns.[1] One of the deities associated with love poetry is Krishna, especially the "Krishna of Gokula, the god brought up among cowherds, the mischievous child, the endearing lover, the eternal paradox of flesh and spirit."[2] Alongside the schools of philosophy in India there developed a "way of devotion." Human devotion to God was compared with various human relationships—between friends, servant and master, child and parent. The most intense form of devotion was seen as analogous to the yearning of separated lovers for one another, as the cowherding women longed for Krishna.

The love between man and woman is a symbolic religious theme in poetry related to Krishna that dates from about 200 C.E. to the present. A classic expression of the theme is found in the tenth book of the *Purana of the Lord*, a collection of various sorts of tradition written in the ninth or tenth century. The devotional songs of the regional saints, written from the fourth century on, also developed the analogy.

---

1. De Bary, *Sources of Indian Tradition*, 1:350.
2. Daniel H. H. Ingalls, in Singer, *Krishna*, v.

In Bengal, the worshippers of Krishna practiced fervent devotion to him in the form of the Lover Supreme. According to their system of thought, the human individual is neither fully separate from nor fully identical with the divine. The greatest quality of the divine is "belovedness." Fully satisfying love, for both lover and beloved, is love for God. Since the individual shares in the divine quality of belovedness, God is attracted to the individual, just as the individual is attracted to God. So the worshipper emulates the love of the cowherding women for Krishna and gives him pleasure, just as Krishna gives pleasure to the worshipper, as he did to the cowherds. Radha is the primary lover of Krishna, and the devotee experiences all the depth of emotion she felt for him.[3]

The following poem is an example of the religious poetry of this movement.[4]

He speaks:

Her slender body like a flash of lightning,
her feet, color of dawn, stepping swiftly
among the other lotus petals....
Friend, tell me who she is! She plays
among her friends,
plays with my heart.
When she raises her eyebrows I see
the arching waves of the River Kālindi.
Her careless look lights on a leaf
and the whole forest flames into blue flowers.
When she smiles
a delicate sweetness fills me, fragrance
of lily and jasmine.

---

3. Edward C. Dimock, "Doctrine and Practice among Vaisnavas of Bengal," in Singer, *Krishna*, 46-49.
4. From Dimock and Levertov, *In Praise of Krishna*, 8.

O Kān [Krishna], you are bewitched:
Do you not know your Rāi [Rādhā]?

This poem is an example of the mood called "the awakening of love between Krishna and Radha." There is a general similarity between it and the Song of Songs. In the Bengali tradition, each poem is spoken either by the male or the female lover. In the Song of Songs, the lovers take turns at speech. Another literary difference is the typical couplet at the end of the Bengali poems, in which the poet comes to speech. An interpretive difference is that, in the Jewish and Christian traditions, the female lover was first understood in a collective sense: the Church or Israel. In the Bengali poems, the female lover represents the individual devotee. This symbolic meaning is similar to an important strand of interpretation in the Christian tradition, in which the female represents the individual soul.

General Bibliography

Aland, Barbara. "A New Instrument and Method for Valuating the Total Manuscript Tradition of the New Testament." In *Bericht der Hermann Kunst-Stiftung zu Forderung der neutestamentlichen Textforschung für die Jahre 1985 bis 1987*. Münster: 1988.

Aland, Kurt, and Barbara Aland. *The Text of the New Testament*. Translated by Erroll F. Rhodes. Grand Rapids, Mich.: Eerdmans, 1987.

Albrektson, B. *"Difficilior lectio probabilior."* *Oudtestamentische Studien* 21 (1981).

Alter, Robert. *The Art of Biblical Narrative*. New York: Basic Books, 1981; Philadelphia: Jewish Publication Society of America, 1983.

Anderson, B. W., ed. *Books of the Bible*. New York: Scribner's Sons, 1989.

Aptowitzer, V. *Kain und Abel in der Agada*. Vienna: R. Löwit Verlag, 1922.

Auvray, P. *Richard Simon 1638-1712: Etude bio-bibliographique avec textes inédits*. Paris: 1974.

Baldermann, Ingo, et al., eds. *Zum Problem des biblischen Kanons*. Jahrbuch für biblische Theologie, vol. 3. Neukirchen-Vluyn: Neukirchener, 1988.

Barr, James. *The Bible and the Modern World*. New York: Harper and Row, 1973.

———. *Holy Scripture: Canon, Authority, Criticism*. Louisville, Ky.: Westminster/John Knox Press, 1983.

———. "Jowett and the Reading of the Bible 'Like Any Other Book.'" *Horizons in Biblical Theology* 4/5 (1982-83): 1-44.

———. *Old and New in Interpretation*. New York: Harper and Row, 1966.

Bassler, J. M. "Cain and Abel in the Palestinian Targums." *Journal for the Study of Judaism* 17 (1986): 56-64.

Barthélemy, Dominique. *Le canon de l'Ancien Testament*. Edited by J.-D. Kaestli and O. Wermelinger. Genève: Labor et Fides, 1984.

———. *Critique textuelle de l'Ancien Testament*. Orbis biblicus et orientalis, vol. 50/1. Fribourg: Presses universitaires, 1982.

———. *Etudes d'histoire du texte de l'Ancien Testament.* Orbis biblicus et orientalis, vol. 21. Fribourg: Presses universitaires, 1978.

Barthélemy, Dominique, D. W. Gooding, J. Lust, and E. Tov. *The Story of David and Goliath: Textual and Literary Criticism: Papers of a Joint Research Venture.* Orbis biblicus et orientalis, vol. 73. Fribourg: Editions universitaires; Göttingen: Vandenhoeck and Ruprecht, 1986.

Bauer, Georg Lorenz. *Theologie des Alten Testaments oder Abriss der religiösen Begriffe der alten Hebräer: Von den ältesten Zeiten bis auf den Anfang der Christlichen Epoche: Zum Gebrauch akademischer Vorlesungen.* 1796.

Baur, Ferdinand Christian. *Vorlesungen über neutestamentliche Theologie.* 1864. Reprint ed. Darmstadt: Wissenschaftliche Buchgesellschaft, 1973.

Beckwith, Roger. *The Old Testament Canon of the New Testament Church and Its Background in Early Judaism.* Grand Rapids, Mich.: Eerdmans, 1985.

Bird, Phylis. "'Male and Female He Created Them': Gen. 1:27b in the Context of the Priestly Account of Creation." *Harvard Theological Review* 74 (1981): 129-59.

Blenkinsopp, Joseph. "Old Testament Theology and the Jewish-Christian Connection." *Journal of the Study of the Old Testament* 28 (1984): 3-15.

———. "Tanakh and the New Testament: A Christian Perspective." In *Biblical Studies: Meeting Ground of Jews and Christians,* edited by L. Boadt, H. Croner, and L. Klenicki, 96-119. Mahwah, N. J.: Paulist Press, 1980.

Boadt, Lawrence, C. S. P., H. Croner, and L. Klenicki, eds. *Biblical Studies: Meeting Ground of Jews and Christians.* Mahwah, N. J.: Paulist Press, 1980.

Bright, John. *A History of Israel.* 3rd ed. Louisville, Ky.: Westminster/John Knox Press, 1981.

Brooks, Roger. "The Problem of Scholarly Ecumenism: The Rabbinic Background for the Study of Origen." In *Origen of Alexandria: His World and his Legacy,* edited by Charles Kannengiesser and William L. Petersen, 63-95. Christianity and Judaism in Antiquity, vol. 1. Notre Dame, Ind.: University of Notre Dame Press, 1988.

Brooten, Bernadette J. *Women Leaders in the Ancient Synagogue: Inscriptional Evidence and Background Issues.* Brown Judaic Series, vol. 8. Decatur, Ga.: Scholars Press, 1982.

Burke, Peter. *The Renaissance Sense of the Past.* New York: St. Martin's Press, 1969.

Buxtorf, J., Jr. *Anticritica . . . adversus L. Cappelli Criticam.* Basel, 1653.

Carr, D. "Royal Ideology and the Technology of Faith: A Comparative Midrash Study of 1 Kings 3:2-15." Ph. D. Dissertation, Claremont Graduate School, 1988.

Childs, Brevard S. *Biblical Theology in Crisis.* Louisville, Ky.: Westminster/John Knox Press, 1970.

————. *Introduction to the Old Testament as Scripture.* Philadelphia: Fortress Press, 1979.

————. *Old Testament Theology in a Canonical Context.* Philadelphia: Fortress Press, 1986.

Clarkson, John F., et al., eds. *The Church Teaches: Documents of the Church in English Translation.* St. Louis: B. Herder, 1955; Rockford, Ill.: Tan Books, 1973.

Cohen, Arthur A., and Paul Mendes-Flohr, eds. *Contemporary Jewish Religious Thought.* New York: Scribner, 1986.

Cohen, M. A. "Record and Revelation: A Jewish Perspective." In *Biblical Studies: Meeting Ground of Jews and Christians,* edited by L. Boadt, H. Croner, and L. Klenicki, 147-71. Mahwah, N. J.: Paulist Press, 1980.

Collins, John J. "Is a Critical Biblical Theology Possible?" In *The Hebrew Bible and Its Interpreters,* edited by B. Halpern and W. Propp. Winona Lake, Ind.: Eisenbrauns, forthcoming.

Colwell, Ernest C. *What is the Best New Testament?* Chicago: University of Chicago Press, 1952.

Crenshaw, James L., ed. *Perspectives on the Hebrew Bible: Essays in Honor of Walter J. Harrelson.* Macon, Ga.: Mercer University Press, 1988.

Cross, Frank Moore. "A New Qumran Biblical Fragment Related to the Original Hebrew Underlying the Septuagint." *Bulletin of the American Schools of Oriental Research* 132 (1953): 15-26.

Cross, Frank Moore, and Shemaryahu Talmon, eds. *Qumran and the History of the Biblical Text.* Cambridge, Mass.: Harvard University Press, 1975.

DeBary, William T., et al., eds. *Sources of Indian Tradition.* 2 vols. 2nd ed. New York: Columbia University Press, 1988.

Dimock, E. C., and D. Levertov, trans. *In Praise of Krishna.* Garden City, N. J.: Doubleday, 1967.

Dorothy, C. "The Books of Esther: Structure, Genre, and Textual Integrity." Ph. D. Dissertation, Claremont Graduate School, 1989.

Douglas, Mary. *Purity and Danger: An Analysis of the Concepts of Pollution and Taboo.* London: Routledge and Kegan Paul, 1966.

Duhaime, Jean. "La doctrine des Esséniens de Qumrân sur l'aprèsmort." In *Essais sur la mort,* edited by Guy Couturier et al., 99-121. Montréal: Fides, 1985.

Dupont-Sommer, A. *The Essene Writings from Qumran.* Oxford: Blackwell, 1961.

Eichrodt, Walther. *Theology of the Old Testament.* 2 vols. Translated by J. Baker. Louisville, Ky.: Westminster/John Knox Press, 1961. Originally published 1933.

Eilberg-Schwartz, Howard. *The Human Will in Judaism: The Mishnah's Philosophy of Intention.* Brown Judaic Studies, vol. 103. Decatur, Ga.: Scholars Press, 1986.

Feld, Edward. "Spinoza the Jew." *Modern Judaism* 9 (1989): 101-19.

Feuer, Lewis Samuel. *Spinoza and the Rise of Liberalism.* Boston: Beacon Press, 1958.

Fischer, Balthasar. *Die Psalmen als Stimme der Kirche.* Edited by A. Heinz. Trier: Paulinus, 1982.

Fish, Stanley. *Is There a Text in this Class? The Authority of Interpretive Communities.* Cambridge, Mass.: Harvard University Press, 1980.

Fishbane, M. *Biblical Interpretation in Ancient Israel.* Oxford: Clarendon Press, 1985.

Fitzmyer, Joseph A. "Historical Criticism: Its Role in Biblical Interpretation and Christian Life." *Theological Studies* 50 (June, 1989): 244-59.

———. "The New Testament at Qumran?" In *The Dead Sea Scrolls: Major Publications and Tools for Study,* 119-23. Society for Biblical

Literature, Sources for Biblical Studies. Decatur, Ga.: Scholars Press, 1977.

Fowler, Robert W. "Post-Modern Biblical Criticism: The Criticism of Pre-Modern Texts in a Post-Critical, Post-Modern, Post-Literate Era." *Proceedings: Eastern Great Lakes and Midwest Biblical Societies,* edited by P. Redditt. Grand Rapids, Mich.: The Societies, 1988.

Fox, Michael V. *The Song of Songs and the Ancient Egyptian Love Songs.* Madison, Wis.: University of Wisconsin Press, 1985.

Frei, Hans W. *The Eclipse of Biblical Narrative.* New Haven and London: Yale University Press, 1974.

Friedman, Richard E., and Hugh G. M. Williamson, eds. *The Future of Biblical Studies: The Hebrew Scriptures.* Semeia Studies. Decatur, Ga.: Scholars Press, 1987.

Frye, Northrop. *The Great Code.* New York: Harcourt Brace Jovanovich, 1981.

Gabler, Johann Philipp. "Oratio de justo discrimine theologiae biblicae et dogmaticae . . . ." 1787.

Gilbert, M. "L'Ecclésiastique: Quel texte? Quelle autorité?" *Revue biblique* 94 (1987): 233-50.

Glatzer, Nahum N. *Hillel the Elder.* Rev. ed. New York: Schocken Books, 1966.

Goldberg, A. "Kain: Sohn der Menschen oder Sohn der Schlange?" *Judaica* 25 (1969): 203-21.

Goldberg, Michael. *Jews and Christians, Getting Our Stories Straight: The Exodus and the Passion-Resurrection.* Nashville, Tenn.: Abingdon Press, 1985.

Goshen-Gottstein, Moshe H. "Christianity, Judaism, and Modern Bible Study." In *Congress Volume Edinburgh, 1974,* 69-88. Vetus Testamentum Supplement, vol. 28. Leiden: E. J. Brill, 1975.

———. "Hebrew Biblical Manuscripts: Their History and Their Place in the HUBP Edition." *Biblica* 48 (1967): 243-90.

———. "*Tanakh* Theology." In *Ancient Israelite Religion: Essays in Honor of Frank Moore Cross,* edited by Patrick D. Miller, Jr., et al., 617-44. Philadelphia: Fortress Press, 1987.

Gottwald, Norman. *The Tribes of YHWH.* Maryknoll, New York: Orbis, 1979.

Greenberg, Moshe. "Exegesis." In *Contemporary Jewish Religious Thought*, edited by Arthur A. Cohen and Paul Mendes-Flohr, 211-18. New York: Scribner, 1986.

———. *On the Bible and Judaism*. Edited by Abraham Shapiro. Tel Aviv: Am Oved.

Greenspahn, Frederick E. "Biblical Scholars, Medieval and Modern." In *Judaic Perspectives on Ancient Israel*, edited by Jacob Neusner, Baruch A. Levine, and Ernest S. Frerichs, 245-58. Philadelphia: Fortress Press, 1987.

Grelot, P. "Les Targums du Pentateuque." *Semitica* 9 (1959): 59-88.

Gunneweg, A. *Understanding the Old Testament*. Old Testament Library. Louisville, Ky.: Westminster/John Knox Press, 1978.

Hanson, Paul D. "Biblical Interpretation: Meeting Place for Jews and Christians." In *Canon, Theology, and Old Testament Interpretation, Essays in Honour of B. S. Childs*, edited by Gene M. Tucker et al. Philadephia: Fortress Press, 1988.

Harl, Marguerite, ed. *La Bible d'Alexandrie, 1. La Genese, traduction du texte grec de la Septante, introduction et notes*. Paris: Cerf, 1986.

Harnack, Adolph von. *Marcion: das Evangelium vom fremden Gott*. Leipzig: J. C. Hinrichs, 1924.

Hartmann, L. "Sirach in Hebrew and in Greek." *Catholic Biblical Quarterly* 43 (1961): 443-51.

Harvey, Van A. *The Historian and the Believer*. New York: Macmillan, 1966.

Heschel, Abraham Joshua. *God in Search of Man: A Philosophy of Judaism*. New York: Farrar, Straus, and Giroux, 1955.

Hurvitz, A. *A Linguistic Study of the Relationship between the Priestly Source and the Book of Ezechiel*. Paris: J. Gabalda, 1982.

Isenberg, S. "An Anti-Sadducee Polemic." *Harvard Theological Review* 63 (1970): 433-44.

Jowett, Benjamin. "On the Interpretation of Scripture." In *The Interpretation of Scripture and Other Essays*, 1-76. London: George Routledge; New York: E. P. Dutton [n. d.].

Kalimi, I. "Three Assumptions about the Kenites." *Zeitschrift für die alttestamentliche Wissenschaft* 100 (1988): 386-93.

Kearns, C. "Ecclesiasticus." In *A New Catholic Commentary on Holy Scripture*, edited by R. Ruller et al. London: Nelson, 1969.

Kennicott, Benjamin. *Vetus Testamentum Hebraicum cum variis lectionibus.* 2 vols. Oxford: 1776-80.

Klopfenstein, M., U. Luz, A. Talmon, and E. Tov, eds. *Mitte der Schrift? Ein jüdisch-christliches Gespräch: Texte des Berner Symposions vom 6. -12. Januar 1985.* Judaica et Christiana, vol. 11. Bern: Peter Lang, 1987.

Knierim, Rolf. "On the Task of Old Testament Theology." *Horizons in Biblical Theology* 6/1 (June, 1984): 25-57; responses, 58-80; Knierim's response, 6/2 (December, 1984): 91-128.

Kravitz, Leonard S. "A Jewish Reading of the New Testament." In *Biblical Studies: Meeting Ground of Jews and Christians,* edited by L. Boadt, H. Croner, and L. Klenicki, 75-95. Mahwah, N. J.: Paulist Press, 1980.

Kugel, James L. "Biblical Studies and Jewish Studies." *Association for Jewish Studies Newsletter* 36 (Fall, 1986): 22.

Lacoque, André. "The 'Old Testament' in the Protestant Tradition." In *Biblical Studies: Meeting Ground of Jews and Christians,* edited by L. Boadt, H. Croner, and L. Klenicki, 120-43. Mahwah, N. J.: Paulist Press, 1980.

Leiman, Sid Z., ed. *The Canon and Masorah of the Hebrew Bible.* New York: KTAV, 1974.

Levenson, Jon D. *Creation and the Persistence of Evil: The Jewish Drama of Divine Omnipotence.* San Francisco: Harper and Row, 1988.

———. "The Eighth Principle of Judaism and the Literary Simultaneity of Scripture." *Journal of Religion* 68 (1988): 205-25.

———. "Hebrew Bible in Colleges and Universities." *Religious Education* 81 (1986): 37-44.

———. "The Hebrew Bible, the Old Testament, and Historical Criticism." In *The Future of Biblical Studies,* edited by Richard E. Friedman and Hugh G. M. Williamson, 19-59. Semeia Studies. Decatur, Ga.: Scholars Press, 1987.

———. *Sinai and Zion.* Minneapolis: Winston, 1985.

———. "Why Jews Are Not Interested in Biblical Theology." In *Judaic Perspectives on Ancient Israel,* edited by Jacob Neusner, Baruch A. Levine, and Ernest S. Frerichs, 281-307. Philadelphia: Fortress Press, 1987.

Levine, E. "The Syriac Version of Gen. IV:1-6." *Vetus Testamentum* 26 (1976): 70-78.

Lindbeck, George. "Scripture, Consensus, and Community." *This World: A Journal of Religion and Public Life* 23 (1988): 5-24.

Lohse, Eduard, ed. *Die Texte aus Qumran*. München: Kosel, 1971.

Machiavelli, Niccolò. *The Prince and the Discourses*. New York: The Modern Library, 1950.

Maier, J. *Die Templerolle vom Toten Meer*. München: Reinhardt, 1978.

Margival, H. *Essai sur Richard Simon et la critique biblique au XVII siècle*. Paris, 1900. Reprint ed. Genève: Slatkine Reprints, 1970.

Mellinkoff, R. *The Sign of Cain*. Berkeley, Calif.: University of California Press, 1981.

Miller, Patrick D., Jr. *Interpreting the Psalms*. Philadelphia: Fortress Press, 1986.

Murphy, Roland E., O. Carm. "Christian Understanding of the Old Testament." *Theology Digest* 18 (1970): 321-32.

———. *Psalms, Job*. Philadelphia: Fortress Press, 1977.

———. "The Relationship between the Testaments." *Catholic Biblical Quarterly* 26 (1964): 349-59.

———. "A Response to 'The Task of Old Testament Theology.'" *Horizons in Biblical Theology* 6/1 (June, 1984): 65-71.

Neusner, Jacob. *Aphrahat and Judaism: The Christian-Jewish Argument in Fourth-Century Iran*. Leiden: E. J. Brill, 1971.

———. *Comparative Midrash: The Plan and Program of Genesis Rabbah and Leviticus Rabbah*. Decatur, Ga.: Scholars Press, 1986.

———. *Formative Judaism*. 2 vols. Brown Judaic Studies, vols. 37, 41. Decatur, Ga.: Scholars Press, 1982; 1983.

———. "History and Structure: The Case of Mishnah's System of Purities." In *Method and Meaning of Ancient Judaism*. Brown Judaic Series, vol. 10. Decatur, Ga.: Scholars Press, 1979.

———. *Judaism: The Evidence of the Mishnah*. Chicago: University of Chicago Press, 1981.

———. *Judaism and Scripture: The Evidence of Leviticus Rabbah*. Chicago Studies in the History of Judaism. Chicago: University of Chicago Press, 1986.

Neusner, Jacob, and William S. Green. *Writing with Scripture: The Authority and Uses of the Hebrew Bible in the Torah of Formative Judaism*. Minneapolis: Fortress Press, 1989.

Neusner, Jacob, Baruch A. Levine, and Ernest S. Frerichs, eds. *Judaic Perspectives on Ancient Israel*. Philadelphia: Fortress Press, 1987.

"Notes on the Correct Way to Present Jews and Judaism in Preaching and Catechesis in the Roman Catholic Church." Vatican Committee for Religious Relations with the Jews. *Origins* 15/7 (July 4, 1985): 102-7; *Osservatore Romano* (June 24, 1985).

Noth, Martin. *Geschichte Israels*. 3rd ed. Göttingen: Vandenhoeck and Ruprecht, 1956. English translation, under the title *The History of Israel: Biblical History*. 2nd ed. New York: Harper and Row, 1960.

Ollenburger, Ben C. "What Krister Stendahl Meant—A Normative Critique of 'Descriptive Biblical Theology.'" *Horizons in Biblical Theology* 8/1 (June, 1986): 61-98.

Popkin, Richard H. *The History of Skepticism from Erasmus to Spinoza*. Rev. ed. Berkeley, Calif.: University of California Press, 1979.

Potok, Chaim. *In the Beginning*. New York: Alfred A. Knopf, 1975.

Rahner, Karl. *Inspiration in the Bible*. Quaestiones Disputatae, vol. 1. 2nd rev. ed. New York: Herder and Herder, 1964.

Rendtorff, Rolf. "Must 'Biblical Theology' Be Christian Theology?" *Biblical Review* 4/3 (June, 1988): 40-43.

———. "'Covenant' as a Structuring Concept in Genesis and Exodus." *Journal of Biblical Literature* 108 (1989): 385-93.

Reventlow, H. Graf. *Problems of Old Testament Theology in the Twentieth Century*. Philadelphia: Fortress Press, 1986.

Rossi, J. B. de. V*ariae lectiones Veteris Testamenti*. 4 vols. Parma, 1784-88.

Sanders, James A. "Adaptable for Life: The Nature and Function of Canon." In *Magnalia Dei: The Mighty Acts of God. Essays in Memory of G. E. Wright*, edited by Frank Moore Cross et al., 531-60. Garden City, N. J.: Doubleday, 1976.

———. *Canon and Community: A Guide to Canonical Criticism*. Philadelphia: Fortress Press, 1984.

———. "The Challenge of Fundamentalism: One God and World Peace." *Impact* 19 (1987): 12-39.

———. "First Testament and Second." *Biblical Theology Bulletin* 17 (1987): 47-49.

———. *From Sacred Story to Sacred Text*. Philadelphia: Fortress Press, 1987.

———. "Text and Canon: Old Testament and New." In *Mélanges Dominique Barthélemy*, edited by P. Casetti et al., 373-94. Orbis biblicus et orientalis, vol. 38. Fribourg: Editions universitaires, 1981.

Sanderson, Judith E. *An Exodus Scroll from Qumran: 4QpaleoExod^m and the Samaritan Tradition.* Harvard Semitic Studies, vol. 30. Decatur, Ga.: Scholars Press, 1986.

Sarna, Nahum M. "The Modern Study of the Bible in the Framework of Jewish Studies." *Proceedings of the Eighth World Congress of Jewish Studies.* Jerusalem: World Union of Jewish Studies, 1983.

Schechter, Solomon. "Higher Criticism—Higher Anti-Semitism." In *Seminary Addresses and Other Papers*, 36-47. Cincinnati: Ark Publishing, 1915.

Simon, Richard. *Histoire critique du Vieux Testament.* Rotterdam: Leers, 1685. Reprint ed. Genève: Slatkine Reprints, 1971.

Singer, Milton, ed. *Krishna: Myths, Rites, and Attitudes.* Chicago: University of Chicago Press, 1966.

Skehan, Patrick W. "Exodus in the Samaritan Recension from Qumran." *Journal of Biblical Literature* 74 (1955): 182-87.

Smend, Rudolf. "Julius Wellhausen and his *Prolegomena to the History of Israel.*" *Semeia* 25 (1983).

Smith, Wilfred Cantwell. "The Study of Religion and the Study of the Bible." *Journal of the American Academy of Religion* 39 (1971).

Soggin, J. Alberto. *A History of Ancient Israel.* Translated by John Bowden. Louisville, Ky.: Westminster/John Knox Press, 1985.

Sperling, S. David. "Judaism and Modern Biblical Research." In *Biblical Studies: Meeting Ground of Jews and Christians*, edited by L. Boadt, H. Croner, and L. Klenicki, 19-44. Mahwah, N. J.: Paulist Press, 1980.

Spinoza, Benedict de. *Tractatus Theologico-Politicus* (1670). Opera: Werke lateinisch und deutsch, edited by G. Gawlick and F. Niewöhner, vol. 1. Darmstadt, 1979. English trans., under the title *A Theologico-Political Tractate and a Political Treatise.* New York: Dover, 1951.

Stade, B. *Geschicte des Volkes Israel.* Berlin, 1899.

Steinmetz, David C. "The Superiority of Pre-Critical Exegesis." *Theology Today* 37 (1980).

Strauss, Leo. *Spinoza's Critique of Religion.* New York: Schocken, 1965.

Sundberg, A. *The Old Testament of the Early Church.* Harvard Theological Studies, vol. 20. Cambridge, Mass.: Harvard University Press, 1964.

Talmon, Shemaryahu. "Heiliges Schrifttum und kanonische Bücher aus jüdischer Sicht—Überlegungen zur Ausbildung der Grösse 'Die Schrift' im Judentum." In *Mitte der Schrift? Ein jüdisch-christliches Gespräch: Texte des Berner Symposions vom 6.-12. Januar 1985,* edited by M. Klopfenstein, U. Luz, S. Talmon, and E. Tov, 45-79. Judaica et Christiana, vol. 11. Bern: Peter Lang, 1987.

———. "The Old Testament Text." In *From the Beginnings to Jerome,* edited by P. R. Ackroyd and C. F. Evans, 159-99. Vol. 1 of *The Cambridge History of the Bible.* Cambridge: Cambridge University Press, 1970.

———. "The Textual Study of the Bible—A New Outlook." In *Qumran and the History of the Biblical Text,* edited by Frank Moore Cross and Shemaryahu Talmon, 321-400. Cambridge, Mass.: Harvard University Press, 1975.

———. "The Three Scrolls of the Law That Were Found in the Temple Court." *Textus (Annual of the Hebrew University Bible Project)* 11 (1962): 14-27.

Tanakh: The Holy Scriptures. The New Jewish Publication Society Translation According to the Traditional Hebrew Text. Philadelphia: Jewish Publication Society of America, 1988.

Tov, Emanuel. "Hebrew Biblical Manuscripts from the Judean Desert: Their Contribution to Textual Criticism." *Journal of Jewish Studies* 39 (1988): 5-37.

———. "Some Aspects of the Textual and Literary History of the Book of Jeremiah." In *Le livre de Jérémie: Le prophète et son milieu, les oracles et leur transmission,* edited by P. M. Bogaert, 145-67. Bibliotheca ephemeridum theologicarum Lovaniensium, vol. 54. Leuven: Leuven University Press, 1981.

Tov, Emanuel, and Johann Cook. "A Computerized Data Base for the Qumran Biblical Scrolls with an Appendix on the Samaritan Pentateuch." *Journal of Northwest Semitic Languages* 12 (1984): 133-37.

Trible, Phylis. *God and the Rhetoric of Sexuality.* Philadelphia: Fortress Press, 1978.

Tsevat, Matityahu. "Theology of the Old Testament—A Jewish View." *Horizons in Biblical Theology* 8/2 (1986): 33-50. (Response by B. W. Anderson, 51-59.)

Ulrich, Eugene. "The Canonical Process, Textual Criticism, and Latter Stages in the Composition of the Bible." In *Festschrift Talmon*, edited by Michael Fishbane and Emanuel Tov. Winona Lake, Ind.: Eisenbrauns, 1990.

―――. "Double Literary Editions of Biblical Narratives and Reflections on Determining the Form to be Translated." In *Perspectives on the Hebrew Bible: Essays in Honor of Walter J. Harrelson*, edited by James L. Crenshaw, 101-16. Macon, Ga.: Mercer University Press, 1988.

―――. "Horizons of Old Testament Textual Research at the Thirtieth Anniversary of Qumran Cave 4." *Christian Biblical Quarterly* 46 (1984): 613-36.

Urbach, Ephraim E. "The Homiletical Interpretations of the Sages and the Expositions of Origen on Canticles, and the Jewish-Christian Disputation." *Scripta Hierosolymitana* 22 (1971): 247-75.

Vermes, Geza. *Post-Biblical Jewish Studies*. Leiden: E. J. Brill, 1975.

von Rad, Gerhard. "Faith Reckoned as Righteousness." In *The Problem of the Hexateuch and other Essays*, 125-30. New York: McGraw-Hill, 1966.

Walters, S. "Hannah and Anna: The Greek and Hebrew Texts of 1 Samuel 1." *Journal of Biblical Literature* 107 (1988): 385-412.

Weinfeld, Moshe. "The Covenant of Grant in the Old Testament and in the Ancient Near East." *Journal of the American Oriental Society* 90 (1970).

Wilken, Robert. *John Chrysostom and the Jews: Rhetoric and Reality in the Late Fourth Century*. Berkeley, Calif.: University of California Press, 1983.

Wright, G. E. *The Old Testament and Theology*. New York: Harper and Row, 1969.

Yovel, Yirmiyahu. "Marrano Patterns in Spinoza." In *Proceedings of the First Italian International Congress on Spinoza*. Naples: Bibliopolis, 1985.

Index of Scriptural Verses

General Index